NO Green Beans

A Woman's Guide to Becoming the Ultimate
5-Course Experience

ATIYA S. STEVENSON

Please contact Art & Legacy Publications for your publishing needs:

www.Artandlegacypublications.com

Endorsements

Atiya S. Stevenson has produced a literary jewel. No Green Beans is a profound and practical guide to any woman fulfilling her self-esteem. it will shift the woman's self-perspective and expectation.

The analogies, in the book, create an immediate visual, and the corresponding principles leave a lasting impression on the soul. No one will read this book and leave the same. No woman could do relationships the same after having consumed the wisdom of this book.

This book should be in the hands of every young and older woman around the world. It structures

R.C. BLAKES
Empowerment Teacher

I recall my visit to a 5-star restaurant while double dating. Once seated, we were offered appetizers of which one person declined and preferred his main course immediately. Therein lies the challenge with most relationships

Women are 5 and 7course meals, but men only desire the main course which is why this book is essential. Atiya lays out the full course woman. If you desire to know how to treat a woman, there's no better person to communicate it other than a woman.

Ladies, when you read this book it will help you understand you are a 5- course experience and will help men to understand how to place their order.

Greg M. Davis
TV/ Radio Personality | Author, When the Right One Comes

No Green Beans by Atiya Stevenson is an exquisite work, masterfully prepared to restore fallen queens and inspire hidden gems. It will surely set a precedent for empowering women of all races and social statuses. This book is as strong and clear as a diamond and as priceless as the women who will be reading it. In short, it is inspirational gold.

In *No Green Beans,* you will discover, there is a grace within each page to build and to assist Ladies in leveling up, to emerge out of the shadows of despair, and to stop settling and embrace the beauty within. Royal Women, you will be challenged to no longer compromise your value system, integrity, and the height to which you have been summoned to sit as Queens. Royal Women, yes, those of you who have lived the pain of being paired with men who could not see beyond thighs, hips, and lips to the treasure you embody, will find strength in these pages to shout "No Green Beans: I am far more than a side chick, booty-call, paycheck, emblem, trophy, and/or a friend with benefits." After examining these pages myself, I am sure that this written work will straighten crowns and improve spiritual, emotional, and mental postures, as Ladies emerge to take their seats, to sit gracefully on their royal thrones of dignity, class, strength, grace, and authority. The table has been set, but you will not find "green beans."

Ron Toliver
CEO - Art & Legacy publications
FOUNDER - Kingdom Revealed Global Alliance

Table of Contents

Endorsements | iii

Table of Contents | v

Acknowledgements | vii

Introduction | 1

The Mantra | 7

Course One: The Appetizer | 9

Chapter 1: The Prerequisite | 11

Surviving Trauma | 21

Chapter 2: Dining Etiquette | 25

Chapter 3: No Shirt ◆ No Shoes ◆ No Service | 35
(The Standard of a Dress Code)

Course Two: The Soup | 41

Chapter 4: What Type of Experience are You? | 43
The "7-Women-to-Every-Man" Myth

Chapter 5: The Wonderful World of Cuisine | 53
"Beware of the Foodie"

Chapter 6: Call the Paramedics - I have Food Poisoning | 63
(Toxic Relationships)

The Palate Cleanser (Intermezzo) | *75*

Chapter 7: The Ultimate Synergy | 77
(Sexuality v Sensuality)

Course Three: The Salad | *89*

Chapter 8: May I Speak with Your Manager Please? | 91
(This is not what I ordered)

Chapter 9: What's your Rating? | 101
"What are people saying?"

Chapter 10: The Boss Chick Movement | 111
"My Concern"

Course Four: The Entrée | *121*

Bonus: Real Men ~ Real Answers | 123

Chapter 11: Braised Artichoke Hearts | 131

Course Five: Dessert | *135*

Chapter 12: "The Power of the "P" | 137

Whipped Cappuccino | 147
(After Dinner Reflection)

Acknowledgements

To "Tia" (aka "Brown Sugar"), the 15-year-old me that was hidden, buried, and misused because I possessed a delicacy of which she had no knowledge.

To "Atiya," the current "me" that has failed, learned, evolved—failed, learned, evolved—failed, learned, evolved--

The "me" that has learned to embrace failure with the liberation that failure is "an event" not "a person."

To my Beautiful Gems & Jewels:

A masterpiece handcrafted with love, touched with grace, housed in strength, created in immaculate imagery, adorned with royalty and poised in femininity.

To my Strong, Resilient, Kings and Priests:

We apologize for not EMBRACING ALL of us so that we can EMBRACE ALL OF YOU!!

The "you" that was taught from adolescence that real men don't cry therefore communication and vulnerability were unheard of.

The "you" that loves just as hard as "we" do but is afraid that you'll be hurt **again!**

The "you" that deep down yearns for a meaningful relationship and simply desires someone to love you through it… even the little boy of whom you have no knowledge, who's trapped inside.

The "you" that wants to love but can't trust due to a foundational betrayal by a biological parent.

The "you" that at your core desires to be held accountable and told "no" and "not yet."

We Honor, Salute, and Esteem You!!

Introduction

Who the heck is Atiya Stevenson? Why did I write this book? ***And what qualifies me to do so? (some may ask).***

One of my revered authors, the late Dr. Myles Munroe, once said, "Where purpose is not known, abuse is inevitable." After decades of error, failure, the blame game, self-deception, and self-sabotage, I recorded memoirs in this writing primarily because I ascribe to the belief that one's journey leads to the path of another.

I'd like to share my awakening moments and what I've learned from them — my "Ah-Ha" moments, my "Girl, how could you be so stupid?" moments, my "How didn't you see that?" moments — my shameful moments when I felt like "leftovers" because I was merely an option to someone who I had made a priority ***on my own accord***.

To my ladies who not only love fine dining but also the ***experience*** that completes the dining—the service, the ambience, the cuisine—take a seat, ladies, and let's chat. This reading is for my beautiful queens, whether you're a 7-figure earner…an 18-year-old who is soul searching…a 45-year-old whose actions don't reflect your inner desire…the divorced woman who's accepted her truth (that her unresolved pain and fear speaks to her)…the woman who is bitter with men, not because she wants to be but because she's not had the courage to accept and learn from her own errors…the woman that's self-deceived and has taught herself to be tough and play the "two-can-play-that-game" cycle as a guard from being misused but doesn't realize that she's already lost when her value was forfeited by her own accord (Game Over).

Disclaimer – This writing is <u>***NOT***</u> to bash or degrade men; as a matter of fact, I love, honor, and respect men. I believe men are Kings and Priests. They are our headship, built to lead and dominate. Candidly speaking, ladies, it is not about men: it's about us, as women, taking responsibility for our actions, whether productive or counterproductive, healthy or self-sabotaging. Furthermore, when we embody the mindset of "All men are dogs" … "I'm gonna play that same game" … "I'm like this because of what **<u>he</u>** did to me," etc., it's self-deception when it should be self-introspection on our part. Subconsciously, we are blaming others for what **<u>we</u>** allow.

It's okay, my love; fret not. Upon the completion of this writing, we will have EVOLVED and will RE-present ourselves as such!! NO GREEN BEANS!!

<u>Who this Reading is for ~ Who will Likely Benefit?</u>

This reading is for my authentic queens who live, or desire to live, their lives from the inside out: precious queens who have hearts made of pure (24-karat) gold. This means although you've been scarred, betrayed, heartbroken-heartbroken-heartbroken, taken for granted, used—rejected by the one you adored, lied to by the one who housed your loyalty, mishandled by the one you held down—my queens (like me), you had to learn from falling and getting back up.

For the one-night stander who was looking for love, the precious gem that basically sold her soul for a luxury car while on cruise control to a dead end. The desire of the designer bag, not realizing that "<u>You</u> are the Label". The one who wanted the Christian Louboutins while your heart and soul bled the same red. The one who vacationed for a piece of his time (and social media) not realizing that "You are a lifetime of an Oasis". The seeker of monetary stability, not realizing that who you are in totality is PRICELESS. The one who believed the lies, manipulation, and deception, not because you were stupid but because you took a chance; the jewels who **were** the liars, manipulators, and deceivers … this is for you also.

My princesses (now queens) who were taught by watching their mothers and other women in their lives play the game to "use what they have to get what they want."

This reading is for my queens who desire to be respected, cherished, adored, and preferred, yet it seems you're reduced and subjected to being an option, a number, a lineup, a subliminal offer, a cash offer, a snack, a string along, or a smash. My beautiful, precious gems, jewels, and queens that lack the courage to do introspection to see the image in the mirror: I mean the image ***PAST*** the image—past the mink lashes, the contour, the bundles, the units, the labels, the status—to look at what seems to be brokenness marred with scars, scorns, and bitterness that seemingly force us to operate in a foreign space, a space that we weren't created to occupy.

The gems that are crazy (I mean sane) enough to, despite the world in which we live, STILL believe that true, meaningful connections exist and that there are men who will not treat you like an event but value you for the lifetime, dimensional experiences that you are. *#NGB*

Who this Reading Isn't For ~ Who will not likely Benefit?

My precious gems, jewels, and queens who are resolved to "doing me" with no consideration of who it affects, this reading may not be for you, initially, however, I still invite you to walk with us through this transformational journey with an open heart and mind, as I was once you. I was not this mean, selfish *(well, yes, I was selfish)*, cold-hearted person, but I lacked the value, wisdom, and courage that living an authentic life from the inside out required of me.

Oh, by the way, sweetheart…that "you" that you're in bondage to is bruised, traumatized, broken, and toxic. There's a much better version of "you" with tons of value and courage of which I'm delighted and committed to aid you in the discovery. *Hugs!*

Woman ~ Who Is She?

Women… Who are we? We are God's BIG Idea! We are God's help (tool) in the earth to assist Men. We are Queens. We are CEOs. We are Mothers. We are Wives. We are Sisters. We are Daughters. We are great Friends. We are Life-givers. We are Incubators. We are visionaries. We can be a rose AND the thorn….

We are beautiful. We come in all shapes, sizes, nationalities, and colors. We have light skin, brown skin, dark skin. We are loyal. We are independent. We are strong. We are resilient. We are durable. We are fearfully, wonderfully, and marvelously made. We are vibrant. We are vivacious. We are brilliant. We are intriguing. We are multi-dimensional. We are graceful. We are colorful. We are elegant. We are intuitive. We are forgiving, we are helpers, We are gifts.

Women are diverse; We can have perfect lining on our full lips or that natural bounce in our curls. Our personalities are vibrant and full of color. The brilliance and innovation of our minds are unparalleled.

We have the ability to take nothing and build it into something extraordinary. We have the strength that not only defies but causes our kings to marvel in a resounding way! We are optimistic. We are opportunists!! You say, "It can't happen?" We say, "Don't believe me, just watch!!"

We have the innate ability to love and forgive until it hurts. We are sensual. We not only see things from afar, but we feel on a level that reaches the deepest depths. We touch the places that one never knew existed. We hear what's not being said and see what's not being shown.

What nudged me to write this book was my evolving, maturation process and passion to see women show up and conquer through understanding their value and worth. My precious jewels, when you truly understand your value, you know that you are priceless!!

Reflecting on dimensions and qualities that women possess, I'd like to share what I've found to be productive when dealing with men and achieving a desired result in a relationship, to be valued for more than just your exterior and performance in the bedroom, or wherever your preference.

As the World Turns

Who remembers "As the World Turns," "The Young and the Restless," and "All My Children" *(my fav)*? They were the infamous world of soap operas, until they were eventually replaced by reality television.

If you've been in tune with our world and the way it has changed and continues to do so, will you agree that a LOT has heightened in the sexual sphere in our music, TV programs, commercials, billboards and with us as QUEENS?!

It's both grieving and disheartening to see what we, *specifically* as women, have appeared to be reduced to in the arena(s) of sexual preference—anywhere from human trafficking, Instagram models, video vixens, arm candy, high class prostitution—seen and desired for our physical features but not heard for the brilliance and depth that we exude.

My beautiful (rare) gems, it's obvious that we have the **vast** ability to bring pleasure, contentment, fulfillment, comfort, peace, acceptance, forgiveness, motivation, solutions, and much more, to our men.

Why the Title ~ No Green Beans?

My heart's desire is that when you conclude the pages of this writing, there will be a greater self-awareness of the vast beauty, the creativity, the gem, the brilliance, the precious commodity, the positive (non-sexual) influence, and the soft unforgettable, irreplaceable femininity that you are draped with—the irreplaceable value of a non-sexual experience!!

In the way of the world today, many allow ourselves to be reduced to an "all-you-can-eat" picked-over buffet, settling for a portion of a man or a dysfunctional counterproductive cycle, not realizing that we house the depth and dimension of a "five-course experience." Instead we show up low value, like a mediocre side of "Green Beans." In some instances, it's glorified because we're laced with Chanel handbags, Christian Louboutins, trips to Dubai, pristine homes/condos, and luxury cars. *NO GREEN BEANS!!*

~The Mantra~

1. I am committed to transformation <u>through</u> self-awareness, authenticity, vulnerability and transparency.
2. I am committed to discovering/rediscovering my value.
3. I am committed to taking responsibility for my own actions and not blaming others.
4. I am committed to speaking only that which GIVES LIFE to myself and others.
5. I am committed to discovering the courage to look within and accept the HARD but LIBERATING TRUTH! It was ME! I was the manipulator.... I was the provoker.... I was the user.... I was the seductress.... I was the plotter.... I was the one who sabotaged.... I was the mistress.... I was the conspirator.... I was the petty one.... I hit below the belt.... I strategized it.... I set him up.... I kept him from his children (for no reason) .... I slept with his friend to get back at him.... You fill in the blank, and if it doesn't apply, then "Let It Fly."
6. I am committed to valuing, forgiving, loving, honoring, and respecting myself.
7. I am committed to valuing, honoring, cherishing, and respecting my body; therefore, I will not allow it to be used, abused, and/or mishandled.
8. I am committed to RECLAIMING the fragments of my soul that I gave away, suppressed, neglected, abandoned, and/or simply ignored.
9. I am committed to respecting all kings and priests in my sphere of influence, as a lifestyle.
10. I am committed to resisting the temptation to allow my influence, affluence, and status deceive me from discovering my truth and where I should make healthy adjustments.

No Green Beans

Course One

※

The Appetizer

A small dish of food or a drink taken *before* a meal or the main course of a meal to *stimulate* one's appetite

10 ∽ *No Green Beans*

Chapter 1
The Prerequisite

pre·req·ui·site
/ˈprēˈrekwəzət/

> *a thing that is required as a prior condition for something else to happen or exist*

What is a prerequisite? As we see in the definition, it's a requirement and contingency for something that is to come. A driver's license is a prerequisite to operating a motor vehicle. A Bachelor's degree is a prerequisite to earning a Master's degree. My precious gems and jewels, the discovery of your value is a prerequisite for showing up in confidence, loving yourself, and getting the ultimate out of connections.

Have you ever wondered where our values derive from? What shapes our idea of self, our esteem, our worth? Our values and beliefs affect our quality of being and our relationships across the board because what you believe is what you experience. The beliefs that we hold are an important part of our identity. Beliefs are critical because they reflect who we are and how we live our everyday lives.

There are three (3) areas surrounding value in which I'd like for you to categorize yourself *(I've already done it)*: We have pronounced (marked, obvious, distinct) value, which is the level of value that is shaped, molded, and nurtured from our time of early/middle childhood and through the stages of adolescence. We have the recovery of value, which is for my jewels who had value but lost it to the hands of someone who stripped it by manipulation, constant betrayal, verbal abuse, psychological abuse, and for some gems and jewels, even domestic abuse. Lastly, we have discovery of value. This, my loves, is for the jewels who have yet to discover how valuable and priceless they really are.

I was there: there was a time when I hadn't discovered my value. How did I know it? Through my actions, I allowed myself to be mishandled and was self-deceived. It was disguised as "Me-doing-Me." It was disguised as me really being interested in someone but quickly turned into basically a casual, sexual "situationship" draped with tangible items.

Gems and jewels, my journey of discovery and rediscovery of my value allowed me to present myself as such. You may ask, "How can one tell if she's yet to discover or rediscover her value?" We can tell by our commitment to self, being totally transparent in assessing our actions, when they scream "low-value," such as chasing men (where you doing all the initiating), giving up our prized possessions way too soon, not allowing a man to see any part of us other than who we are in bed, basically begging him to stay, and having no boundaries (anything goes).

My loves, do you know that men can detect women of value and the lack thereof?

My loves, do you know that men can detect women of value and the lack thereof? They can detect low self-esteem. They can detect when we're thirsty *(which turns men off)* and when we're easy. Do you realize that our value or lack thereof is even found in our eyes? The way we walk, the way we hold our head when we speak, the way we communicate?

I personally walk with my head held high because I'm confident in who I am. When you walk with confidence, it speaks, ladies. It says, "I know my worth." My countenance is bright, it's cheerful, it's welcoming, it's strong. I didn't say "masculine" I said strong. You can be draped in femininity and still have a strong personality that translates to "I mean business, and I'm not to be played with."

Gems, another prerequisite is "respect" for yourself and for others. To intentionally disrespect others is a trait of a lower version of self. When we disrespect our sisters, it, too, is a trait of our lower self because the way we treat others is a reflection of who we are internally. When one must tear someone else down to make herself feel esteemed, it's a definite version of lower self.

Gems, I've come to realize that discovering one's worth is not automatic, easy, and certainly isn't instant. As we said earlier, value must first be identified, shaped, and nurtured. It doesn't start where we are, precious queens; if it did, we wouldn't have those times as adult women when we say to ourselves, "Why can't I break this? ... Why can't I leave him alone? ... Why do I keep allowing myself to be mishandled?"

Our value actually begins when we are precious little girls—you know, the little princesses with the bows? The little girls whose fathers told us how beautiful we were…or maybe not. Our fathers who protected, provided, affirmed, taught, and cultivated us…or maybe not. The picture that was painted by how our fathers treated our mothers with honor, esteem, and respect…or maybe not. Our fathers who took us on dates at 6 years old, opened doors for us, and bought us flowers...or maybe not.

A positive father-daughter relationship can have a huge impact on a young girl's life and even determines whether she develops into a strong, confident woman. A father's influence in his daughter's life shapes her self-esteem, self-image, confidence, and opinions of men. Fathers play a key role in the psychological development of their daughters from the moment that they are born. When fathers are present and loving, their daughters develop a strong sense of self and are more confident in their abilities. In order to develop positive self-esteem, a healthy father-daughter bond is key. Whether it is with a father, stepfather, grandfather, uncle, big brother, or all of the above, a healthy bond with a male presence is critical for a girl—and even a woman.

My loves, our relationships with our dads (or the lack thereof) are critical to our perception of love, value, and men. The photographic image of what our homes looked like plays an enormous role in who we are today. If your father was absent...you never knew him... he was not in the home...he was present but absent...or maybe he was there, all played a huge part in your life and grounded you with the mental, emotional, and physical stability needed. If Dad was not there, then that critical segment of life is missing and subconsciously affects us and contributes to the women we are today.

In many cases (not all), we were reared without the affirmation of our fathers. We lack the identity that comes from a father figure.

A father's influence in his daughter's life shapes her self-esteem, self-image, confidence, and opinions of men.

When we lack the identity that comes from a father figure, not only does it obscure our vision of self, but it also causes us to lack the understanding of a man's presence and how it translates in our lives. As a result, we never see the value or the necessity of a man.

There are some of us jewels who have jaded perspectives of men, whether it is because our mothers, grandmothers, sisters, aunties, or even ourselves suffered verbal, psychological, and/or physical abuse. Though I'm not a mental health professional, I read and enjoy content about different levels of abuse and its affects. According to *Psychology Today*, when a woman is abused by a man, subconsciously and over time, the woman begins to feel worthless and as if she deserved it. Imagine as a young child, you witnessed or were a victim of abuse; it shapes your beliefs about love.

Some of us were manipulated, meaning that we were mishandled and then bought very nice gifts, so what does that teach us? In our adult relationships that teaches us that it's okay for us to be mishandled and disrespected by men—it's okay for us to be cheated on, devalued, and spoken to in an inappropriate manner, as long as he's taking care everything financially and the makeup sex is out of this world.

These beliefs and behaviors cause psychological trauma, which is toxic and forms a dysfunctional cycle. Some of us, precious queens, have locked away our pain and thrown away the key. So here we are, full-grown in one area and a five-year-old little girl in another. Why? Because we never really grew emotionally from our last point of trauma (shock, disturbance, suffering). Trauma can affect us in so many ways, and oftentimes we suppress it, cross our fingers, and hope it goes away because the pain that accompanies it is sometimes unbearable. My gem, trauma doesn't just go away; it actually finds a comfortable, resting place in the basement of our souls where we left it. The only way to get through it is to first face it, process through it, and conquer (defeat) it.

It's unfortunate and disheartening that many of us have suffered sexual and physical abuse. My heart hurts that you have endured that. Gems and jewels, please hear me: My primary purpose for writing this manuscript is not to say I've written a book but rather to connect with you through these pages. If we never meet in person, I want you to know that you are valuable—you are worthy and deserving of meeting the most amazing woman in the world, which is you! You are deserving of someone who will see your value and love, honor, cherish, and adore you.

I want you to know that you matter: you are an ultimate, 5-course experience, not merely a side of green beans. My desire and challenge for you is to discover your worth, position your worth, and present your worth. My desire and challenge are for you to take the necessary time to address any internal trauma in your life (past and present) that you've neglected, suppressed and/or ignored and to accept it for what it is so that you can be healed. My desire and challenge for you are to spend time with "you," get to know "you," and embrace that jewel that is in you!

You are deserving of someone who will see your value and love, honor, cherish, and adore you.

My desire and challenge for you is to discover your confidence: the confidence that demands happiness, success, and great relationships! When we show up with a level of confidence, we are better able to handle situations, obstacles, frustrations, and the like.

Gems, let's be honest: some of us didn't learn confidence growing up. We didn't get it from our parents, but we decided that we <u>will</u> give to our children. We were never taught the importance of not giving up. We were never taught how to value ourselves. Therefore, we had to learn in the school of hard knocks *(both hands raised)*.

I've intentionally taken the time to lay a strong, deep foundation of prerequisites because we are only as strong as our roots, not our branches. Everything we'll explore as we journey through these transformational pages will refer to these prerequisites. Jewels, you will hear me reiterate again, and again, and again about value and the lack thereof. Why? Because I'm a testament (witness) that when we understand our worth, there are just certain things we cannot and will not allow in our lives.

I understand that I am not to be compared to anyone because I'm incomparable (unique, unparalleled, unsurpassed). So are you! We are not better than anyone else; we're just affirmed in who we are, which is a beautiful thing. I'm sure you will agree that we are laying an intense foundation here, and that is correct because we are committed to intense results.

When we reference the "Ultimate 5-Course Experience," we are primarily speaking of a holistic (all-inclusive) woman. Gems and jewels, for us to be holistic, we must be healed of trauma. It affects our relationships, how we show up, how we view ourselves, and ultimately how we view others. Experiencing trauma (rejection, abandonment, neglect, etc.) has a way of making us feel victimized every day of our lives. It could have happened years ago, but because we've not acknowledged and dealt with it, it's dealing with us in some way or another. It comes out in our relationships, the way we raise our children, our work, and other areas of our lives.

For some of us, trauma causes an unstable existence because there's no emotional stability. Generally, when we've grown up in emotionally stable homes, we've received the love and attention needed, and we have a healthy balance in other relationships. On the contrary, if we've been rejected by caregivers—they were nonresponsive or just not around—emotional trauma is created and, as a result, affects our relationships: we are more than likely to avoid close relationships ... we can't get emotionally close to anyone ... We can have sex or do casual, but there's no emotional attachment ...

This, my jewels, is the engine beneath the hood that drives us to present "the side of green beans." We're self-deceived and masked, and it seemingly doesn't bother us. However, at our core (the basement), we do desire. Our capacity has been altered due to our primary and foundational structures being compromised by a parent, caretaker, etc. Excessive trauma can cause us to be fearful and even delusional of relationships but simultaneously not wanting to be alone, so we take what we can get.

My loves, inner healing is not only critical for growth but liberates the soul. Ladies, we were designed for relationships, connections, love and partnership. When we have casual sex, it causes us to "detach" from who we are, our femininity, and our vulnerability. If there are no boundaries, then casual sex and "situationships" are no longer occasional but become the norm. My precious, sacred gems and jewels, with this pattern of behavior, it's highly unlikely that the men we desire will mutually desire us as a wife or a partner, but rather as "a side of green beans," a jump-off, or an option.

This isn't to say that we aren't worth it, but the way we are presenting ourselves is what matters and speaks. Gems, I challenge you to discover the best in you, so you can <u>present</u> the best of you. A lot of times, we present the rest of us—the rest of us after unresolved trauma, the rest of us after numerous break ups (with no time to heal), the rest of us after unhealthy balances and boundaries. After a while, pieces of you are here, there, and everywhere. Why? Because that's where the pieces of you were left. I challenge you, my love, to RECLAIM yourself!

Unresolved trauma can also lead to self-sabotaging in relationships. I'll be the first to say that love is a risk. Being involved with someone is risk. We risk the chance of being vulnerable; we risk the chance of being rejected; we risk the chance of getting too close to someone unintentionally.

When self-sabotage happens, it can, oftentimes, be traced back to a level of trauma that caused insecurity, inferiority, etc. Oftentimes, self-sabotage happens when a person has had bad experiences in prior relationships, either romantic or familial. When things go well, they may feel like they don't deserve it or that something is wrong, so they cut it off, talk themselves out of it, or not allow themselves to be vulnerable.

Another prerequisite is accountability. You are valuable and should be handled as such. For some, we have allowed others (including men) to handle us as they wished, which oftentimes concluded in our being mishandled. Remember... some men will test us to see what we allow, period!

Gems, I am committed and resolved to being an instrumental tool that brings holistic healing to women. While writing this manuscript, I knew that it would be transformational and cause women to stumble upon areas where assistance would be needed to walk through. While signature and elite coaching is available to accompany this book, I also wanted to have a resource available should one desire professional therapy in the journey of discovering; hence, we've partnered with a licensed mental health professional who has insight and expertise with women and trauma.

20 ⮠ *No Green Beans*

Surviving Trauma

LaBreyia J. Ellis, MS, CLPT

Surviving trauma is like walking through life with a shattered pair of glasses. You can see and experience life, but your perception and vision are fragmented. A deeply distressing or disturbing experience, better known as trauma, impacts more than you could imagine. Trauma can include witnessing or being the victim of violence, tragic loss, and abuse (emotional, physical, psychological, sexual and/or verbal). More concealed versions of trauma include—but are not limited to—house fires, homelessness, lack of affection from parental figures, witnessing family fights, absence of a parent, and battling illness. These events leave imprints on our brain and impact its proper function.

Trauma, great or small, has an overwhelming impact on relationships within ourselves, family, friends, co-workers, and especially our romantic partners. Our spouses or significant others are on the front line, receiving all that we have experienced and have been taught in life *(bless their hearts)*! When we decide to commit to relationships, our counterparts are exposed to and effected by how we communicate and resolve conflict. They also witness the impact of how we respond to pressure, failure, loss, danger, and love.

Untreated trauma causes us to expect danger, betrayal, and question our safety, prohibiting true intimacy and trust in those with whom we share our lives. It can create difficulty in emotional regulation, leaving us unable to notice the warning signs, articulate how we feel, and cope with our affect.

I remember meeting a woman who, for most of her childhood, witnessed her mother in an abusive relationship, leaving her feeling helpless, angry, and eventually numb. She would self-isolate to keep herself safe from the daily impact. Years later, desiring her own relationship, she struggled with emoting due to years of practiced numbness, thus impacting her ability to open up to a man of interest. Did she encounter an abusive mate? No. However, the fear of a potential threat crippled her openness to receive love for years on end and was evidenced by low self-esteem and idle speculations of infidelity.

What about that young lady who is raising her siblings due to an overworked mother and encounters rape by a family member? She is groomed to "just take care of it," like she does with her siblings. Consequently, she buries her trauma of neglect and abuse, pushing the blame inward as only a caretaker can. Now a married woman, she has difficulty regulating her emotions because she has learned to take care of others rather than attune to her own affect. Unable to communicate her needs and boundaries, she has learned to over-function in relationships. She resents her husband for not doing enough in the home and resents her boss who depends on her proficiency but will not compensate her fairly. Bitter and burnt-out, she has no desire for sex, and when it does occur, she experiences flashbacks from her sexual trauma.

We all have survived something. We all are making the best of our circumstances. However, taking the time to admit yourself to the hospital and undergoing surgery to stop the internal bleeding is left for those who desire wholeness, wellness, and abundance. Why walk through life with a limp when you can strut through life to ensure that crown does not fall? Yet if/when it does you have the tools to recover with grace.

Trauma is not a death sentence, but investing time to heal lends to insight, self-awareness, effective communication, and coping skills. Transparency in your journey can lead to life-changing impact and a blue-print for other queens like yourself.

LaBreyia Ellis is a Licensed Professional Counselor with a passion to walk the journey of healing through traditional and Christian counseling. In November 2018, she opened The Intentional Wellness Group, LLC, a private practice counseling center in Lafayette Hill, Pennsylvania. She counsels teens, women, couples, and families to overcome anxiety, depression, trauma, and relational discord. LaBreyia holds a Bachelor's of Arts in Psychology from Bethune-Cookman University and a Master's of Arts in Clinical and Community Counseling from Eastern University. She is a wife and a mother of two beautiful children. Her mission is to break the stigma of mental health in the lives of minorities and followers of Christ.

Website: www.Myiwgroup.com

Instagram: @IntentionalWellnessgrp

24 ∽ *No Green Beans*

Chapter 2
Dining Etiquette

et·i·quette
/ˈedəkət,ˈedəˌket/

> *the conduct or procedure required by good breeding or prescribed by authority to be observed in social or official life*

Please don't speak with food in your mouth … Don't begin your meal until the guest of honor has begun … Silence your cell phone before sitting down … Elbows off the table … oh, and please leave your dinner napkin should you leave the table during your meal.

Etiquette is defined as the formal manners and rules that are followed in social or professional settings.

Here are the silverware and dinnerware rules: Eat to your left; drink to your right. Any **food** dish to the left is yours, and any glass to the right is yours. Start with the knife, fork, or spoon that is farthest from your plate; work your way in, using one utensil for each course.

My incomparable jewels, if there's etiquette when using utensils, certainly there should be etiquette when encountering a delicacy such as you: The Ultimate 5-Course Experience!

In a fine dining setting, reservations aren't optional, they are required. This is primarily for one reason: to uphold the establishment's value of excellence. You will never arrive to a fine dining establishment and find numerous guests waiting to be seated. Why? Because their standards of excellence are to prepare and accommodate as parts of the elevated dining experience. There's something about arriving at an establishment and your arrival is expected and planned. *Mr. Jones? Right this way please.*

Jewels, we should understand the importance of someone planning for us. If you are dating, or even in a relationship, it's okay—and actually should be expected—for the man to prepare and plan sometimes. If you're asked out, then the accommodations should be in place. You shouldn't be asked to "pick a spot." It's okay to ask what type of cuisine you prefer, but the date should be planned by the one who asks. Why is this important? It's important because not only is it etiquette, but it also allows you to observe the type of man with whom you are dealing.

I believe there are things that men should still execute, men should open and close doors, men should pull out chairs, men should remove and put on coats, men should walk closest to the curb, men should make you feel safe and protected when you're in their presence. My loves, the only way you can **expect** something is that you must know **what** to expect *(remember our prerequisites)*. I don't believe chivalry is dead. I believe there are still men who are likened to knights that are loyal, courteous, protective, honorable, gentle, courageous and humble — men that seek a true, deep, and lasting **love** and connection.

I must interject here and say, precious gem, that chivalrous man desires and requires the "Ultimate 5-Course Experience" woman. A chivalrous man wouldn't pursue a woman that serves "green beans only" and would likely decline her sexual advances. This dispels the myth that all men want is sex. I must agree that all men want sex, but it's not all they want.

I'm wondering if women presented more of the "Ultimate 5-Ccourse Experience," would men desire more of the woman in totality? *(See chapter – Sex is overrated and undervalued)*

Valet parking is an accommodation that allows the comfort and convenience of having your vehicle parked and monitored while you are dining. Some valets are complimentary for guests, while others are a paid service. Although valet parking is an option, some would rather self-park and walk; others prefer the accommodation and convenience of entering the restaurant on arrival.

Jewels, as we continue to explore the necessity of preparing, please understand that you are worthy. You are worth the additional expense for the accommodation. Please don't allow yourself to be self-parked on the 3rd level of the parking garage because someone else feels you're not worth the minimal expense to make things right for you. Please don't misinterpret and minimize what I'm saying by placing emphasis on a dollar amount. Some women may say, "It doesn't matter whether we valet or self-park," and that's totally fine. However, my goal for metaphorically using "Valet" is to reiterate your worth and the importance of a man making accommodations or his lack thereof.

I believe there are still men who are likened to knights that are loyal, courteous, protective, honorable, gentle, courageous and humble

In dining etiquette, one must _**wait**_ to be seated; it's not customary to grab the first seat you see. Because reservations have been made prior, your arrival is expected and anticipated. Therefore, the Maître d', host, or server escorts you to your area, whether private, balcony, or dining room seating it has been prepared for your arrival.

Ladies, ladies, ladies…let's chat about "Navigation" for a moment and how it relates to the previous mention of a man making preparation for you. Gems, we are on the move! We make things happen … we're superwomen … we're multi-taskers … want it done, give it to us … Some of us may even push you to the side if you're not moving fast enough! *(lol)* We can't help it: it's our nature.

However, my loves, when our "get-it-done" nature isn't leveraged properly, it can be to our disadvantage, especially with our kings and priests. "How so?" you might ask. Oftentimes, men are wired to "go with the flow." Let's say you meet someone, and you come out of the gate full speed ahead: you're planning everything … you're making all the suggestions … you're always the one reaching out first … you're always on the offense when you should intentionally fall back and be on the defense. Jewels, it is important to allow the man to navigate/drive. *(See next chapter.)* When you allow him to navigate, you're able to assess *(our fav)* with more precision. You're able to assess his level of interest, whether he's **initiating** or responding.

I'm not speaking of playing childish games and making him chase you. In fact, I believe at some point you should slow down or even "stop" in an effort to be captured, if the feeling is mutual. Yes, we want men to show their interest; however, men desire the same, or they will stop pursuing because it's not being reciprocated. Clearly, the "Ultimate 5-Course Experience" would never mislead anyone because she treats others how she would like to be treated. ☺

Alright my loves, you've arrived at your prepared place for dining, and you enter doors and proceed to the hostess where your reservations are confirmed. You're escorted to your cozy table for 2, where the ambience of sultry songs fills the atmosphere, the flickering of candlelight dims the room, and the intimacy of the atmosphere is pregnant with possibilities. Your captivating company for the evening pulls out your chair and nestles you in; you feel the breeze of his Creed cologne as he takes his seat. Your server arrives, greets you with elevated hospitality, lays your napkin in your lap, and suggests the wine, cocktails, and appetizers for the evening.

You and your company for the evening have reviewed the menu together and have discussed what's interesting and what you'll decline. It's now time to place your order, and your server is in position. It's your turn to order, and as you submit your request, you're realizing two things: a vast majority of the menu items are those that you've not seen before, also with all the apostrophes, the pronunciations of your preferred dishes aren't familiar to you. There's nothing more uncomfortable and uneasy that mispronunciation of menu items.

Did you know there's a tactful way (dining etiquette) that you can ask for clarity of a dish without pronouncing it? My jewels, I suggest you research it because after all "You" are the "Ultimate 5-Course Experience," and you more than anyone should be able to properly "pronounce" what's available on "your" menu.

Gems, you must know your menu and have clear "pronunciation" of it, which translates to how you communicate your worth to others! Know your value because…guess what, my love? If you aren't crystal clear about what your menu serves, then you give others (including men) no other option but to name you what they desire because they aren't able to pronounce (speak, utter, articulate) the dimension of the woman that you are. Your menu should be clear and concise. "Pronunciation" is critical because it determines whether you and someone else are speaking the same language. It's your responsibility as a woman to introduce the man to your menu (experience) and then show him how to place his order. You create the menu—you layout the menu.

Your selections are submitted as you warm into the ambience, the evening, and one another. As the experience continues, the server returns with an oshibori (おしぼり or お絞り) if dining Japanese, or hot towel in English, which is a wet **hand towel** offered to clean one's hands before dining. It's now time for the appetizer tasting, and the server brings out an array of house specialties. You reach for closest (first) fork in sight: the one allotted for the main course—after all, how would you know which to use when there are 4 surrounding your plate?

As the evening, conversation, and discovery progress, several courses in the dining experience are served that elevate towards the main course meal. As you view the table setting sample below, you'll see that each meal course is accompanied with an exclusive utensil. My loves, it's imperative that first you are acclimated with fine dining and what utensils are to be used. Then, you can communicate "Dining Etiquette" to others (with clarity) when they attempt to reach for the main course utensil and are beginning with appetizers.

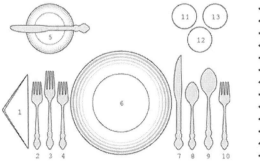

- Napkin (1)
- Salad fork (2)
- Dinner fork (3)
- Dessert fork (4)
- Bread and butter plate, with butter knife (5)
- Dinner plate (6)
- Dinner knife (7)
- Teaspoon (8)
- Soup spoon (9)
- Cocktail fork (10)
- Water glass (11)
- Red wine glass (12)
- White wine glass (13)

There is a purpose for why a formal table setting is as such. They are arrayed for the accommodation of working from the outside inward. If you notice, the cocktail/appetizer fork isn't even on the same side as the main course because, my loves, the time allotted between the appetizer and the main course should be the process in which you should be giving a "non-sexual taste" of your experience. You should be presenting your indispensable, non-sexual qualities.

My primary purpose for including a formal table setting is to give a visual and explanation of the levels and dimensions in which you are housed as a woman. Each utensil is intentionally placed to be utilized as part of the "Ultimate 5-Course Experience." There isn't just one fork, one spoon, and one knife; remember, we're not a café or buffet—we are a 5-star ultimate dining experience. The utensils and their positioning indicate the various delicacies that are offered. What am I saying? My loves, each dimension of who you are should be exclusive and inclusive of an experience. There's no need to re-use utensils because what was needed during the last course may not be needed for the next *(wink)*.

Also, it prevents "overuse": when others are allowed to partake of a specific portion of you ("green beans") without any desire or appetite for the full course experience, which is your mind, your beautiful soul, your thought process, your gift, or your presence—all of the other non-sexual qualities with which you are arrayed. Oh, and as a reminder, overuse is misuse. Each area of your existence should be a "discovered" dimension of you in a brand-new

Each area of your existence should be a "discovered" dimension of you in a brand-new way: You are a world-class woman!

way: You are a world-class woman! But the only way you can present it is if you first understand that you possess it! #*NGB* #*Theultimate5courseexperience*

Therefore, allowing yourself to be an "Ultimate 5-Course Experience" is critical because you determine what part of the course is available by what you present. Only the course that is being consumed should be accessible. Remember, my love, you are being discovered on a need-to-know basis. Some men may not even make it past the glass of wine or the appetizer, and that's okay. It's the advantage of being the "Ultimate Experience" and having a systematic approach in place, which is translated to assessments and boundaries. It's okay if it doesn't work out; at least you didn't allow them to barge in and consume the "green beans" first *(wink)*.

Remember, gems, if "green beans" are the extent of your menu, there's no variety, that's the only choice from which he has to choose. Regardless of how they are prepared, they are still green beans. However, if you present a variety of value (your other attributes), you've given him more to choose from that's already "included" in the experience. *Why, I'm an experience, a package deal.* There's no à la carte available; you can't pick and choose. Be the inclusive woman, meaning the value of who you are comes in a package.

Additionally, the man with whom you're dealing should have an appetite, desire, and patience for the experience of a full course meal and not the drive-thru that serves cold chicken nuggets 24 hours a day. The 5-course, world-class woman has the ability to assess (evaluate) through time and attention, when a man's palate (appetite, taste) is accustomed to fine dining simply by his "etiquette" (behavior). If he speaks with his mouth full…no etiquette. If he lacks proper pronunciation of the menu (you)…no etiquette. If he's not interested in the appetizer, soup, salad, or desert, only the main course…no etiquette. His palate is adjusted to buffets, cafes, and the drive-thru. This, my love, has nothing to do you with you. To reiterate… some men just aren't ready—*#period*.

34 ~ *No Green Beans*

Chapter 3

No Shirt ◆ No Shoes ◆ No Service

(The Standard of a Dress Code)

"What's the occasion?" and "What's the attire?" are my primary questions if I'm invited to an event. Why are they important? You'll want to know the occasion in an effort to bring a gift that is commensurate, and you'll want to know the attire so that you dress appropriately and won't look or feel out of place. If you're invited to an all-white bridal shower brunch, it wouldn't be proper etiquette to wear red and bring a baby bassinet as a gift.

Etiquette is critical; it maintains and preserves the value of the occasion and/or experience. As we continue to discover "etiquette," we learn that some have it, some don't, and some don't have a clue as to what it is. Gems, as a result, our foundation is built upon the commitment to self, assessment of others, and transparency…to name a few.

A dress code is extremely important wherever you are—you clearly wouldn't wear a cocktail dress to a football game! A dress code establishes a standard, and it also distinguishes. Many fine dining restaurants have a dress code standard. You can't walk in with shorts and flip flops, why? Because of the standard they've established for their value and brand. They understand what they represent; their experience is different from anyone else's. Therefore, a standard is required.

Jewels, establishing a standard is just as important when meeting someone and dating. Your standard and boundaries are critical when getting to know someone, not just for you, but for them also. The man who is pursuing you deserves the opportunity to experience "your" experience: introduce yourself, my love. Contrary to what we think, men actually appreciate standards and boundaries in women.

It's what separates us. It doesn't matter what other restaurants (relationships) he's frequented; when he dines with you, there's a standard <u>and</u> an experience. He's intrigued yet motivated: intrigued by the "course" you've presented and motivated to know more! What makes him motivated to know more? You provided "dining etiquette" … you didn't allow yourself to be consumed in one setting … you established boundaries, and your standard required a dress code. My love, <u>this</u> is what changes the game—this is what makes you an exclusive.

Jewels, your standard and boundaries are your non-negotiables; if you've not created any, may I strongly suggest that you do so, please? A non-negotiable is something (or several things) that you absolutely cannot and will not deal with when dating or in relationship: there is no compromise.

Please understand, my love, that a non-negotiable is not the same as making an adjustment *(which I think should be made in partnerships)*. A non-negotiable could be that you won't date a man with children because you don't have any or you won't date a man who smokes because you dislike the smell in clothes, the car, on his breath, etc. An adjustment could be that we're going to the movies and he prefers an action movie, but I prefer a comedy; either of us can make an "adjustment" to appease the other.

Your non-negotiable is your standard based upon your self-worth. Some women's standard may be to not kiss a guy until the 5th date.

Some women may be resolved in saving themselves sexually until they are married. Other women have religious values, and so forth.

Gems, another aspect of standard is the importance of being "slow-cooked-to-perfection." It's critical, ladies, that you allow yourself to be reserved and simmer on low. It's not dining etiquette to be "turned-up" when presenting yourself as an "Ultimate 5-Course Experience." Don't allow a man to barge in full speed ahead, with no boundaries or etiquette, taking what he wants when he wants it. Remember, you are the "5-Course Experience," and you serve how you would like to show up. While it's okay for him to know what he wants, you must assess his level of intentionality and consistency.

When you allow the man to navigate, it enables you to determine his destination (intentions) and assess his ability to take the lead, all while relaxing and going for the ride.

The reason we are making assessment in this area is because it's needed. Ladies, always, always, always allow the man to navigate the course you are on. Now of course, it's your choice to decide if you will remain in the car.

When you allow the man to navigate, it enables you to determine his destination (intentions) and assess his ability to take the lead, all while relaxing and going for the ride. Gems, this is a critical aspect that is oftentimes overlooked. Let's explore a few settings in a navigation system (or global positioning system—GPS).

One thing I've learned is to always allow sufficient time for travel. Your average travel time may be 30 minutes, but due to unforeseen circumstances such as an accident, traffic, etc., your travel time may be prolonged. So, what was to be 30 minutes is now over an hour. Ladies, watch carefully, don't allow anyone to put you on pause or in a holding pattern because of other things going on with them. Don't allow yourself to be delayed. You've been seeing him for almost a year sexually and every other way, yet there's a delay in commitment. My precious jewel, please exit the car! #Nogreenbeans

One thing that completely gets under my three daughters' skin is when I'm preoccupied while driving, having a conversation and following navigation all at the same time! *(I know I know)* The reason they're frustrated is because when all of the above are happening simultaneously, I'm distracted in one way or another, which oftentimes concludes with me missing the exit *(lol)*. I can always tell when I've missed it because I'll hear sighs from my girls, as well as "You've been rerouted" interrupting through the speaker. When this happens, being rerouted always results in longer travel times.

My precious jewels, please don't allow yourself to constantly be rerouted because the driver is distracted with too many other things, resulting in never getting to the destination in the allotted time. He's prevented from giving the necessary attention because he's comfortable in his ability to drive (dealing with women) but overlooking the fact that he's never been on this route before (your experience. Ladies, we must assess!

We must realize that some men must be taught (not trained—men aren't dogs) how to handle you. Oftentimes, all of us are grouped together until we separate and differentiate ourselves, which requires that he takes the proper time to be attentive to you, your needs, your personality, your vibe, <u>your experience.</u>

I can recall when I was 18 years old and had a roughneck boyfriend named Tahir *(lol)*. I mean, he was a roughneck! I remember, as if it was yesterday, driving on the expressway traveling from one end of city to the other. As he accelerated to at least 80-85 mph, swerving, I pleaded with him to slow down! I literally saw my life flash before me. He was clearly driving recklessly. Had anything tragic happened *(thank God it didn't)*, we both would have been casualties, as his actions affected me also.

What am I saying? Ladies, some men are reckless (irresponsible, wild, thoughtless, uncontrolled); they are reckless in their actions, how they handle themselves and others, and how they handle you. Safeguard yourself from allowing men to barge into your space full speed ahead. If a vehicle is driven too fast by a careless, negligent driver, a tragedy is bound to happen. You're at risk due to the driver's lack of concern or capacity to care for his/her own life, which is obviously minimal to none. *#NGB #Please #Exit #The #Car*

Have you ever been lost without a GPS? *I have!* You're looking for a place to make a safe U-turn—one that will get you on the same route prior to the detour without any additional delays. There's nothing like thinking you're on your way to safety after you've been lost. You're looking for a stop light, a store, a strip mall, something that says you're somewhat on the right track. You're hopes are up as you continue the journey and anticipate finally arriving to your destination—when all of a sudden you see the words "Dead End." You're frustrated and disappointed at this point. You want to get to your destination, and despite your anticipation and even the landmarks that seemingly led you in the right direction, you must now turn around because the road you were traveling isn't going anywhere. It's not a through street.

Precious jewels don't find yourself in a dead-end situation. Please assess, ladies. Don't allow yourself to be driven all around with no destination; he has no desire for a committed relationship, and what you have isn't going anywhere. Sure, he'll show you around and give you just enough to keep you anticipating and staying in the car; however, a few miles up the road is a *#DeadEnd #NGB #Please #Exit #The #Car.*

My loves, I admonish you to please take time to properly assess and prevent the mistake of not only **driving the car** but also making the **assumption** that both of you are going in the same direction because he's **in** the car. Queens, there's a difference between a man **driving the car** and a man **riding "shotgun."** When he rides shotgun, he's in the passenger seat, basically going where *you* take him. He's going with the flow; however, *you* are driving the relationship. Do you only hear from him **in response** to your initiation? … Is the only time you spend time together when *you* are contacting him and making plans? … Is he acquainted with your entire family, but you know absolutely no one except a few of his friends? Queens, we must pay attention. This critical area will cause a lot of us to be upset and blame the man because we feel we're being misled, when in fact, my love, you misappropriated: he was never leading—you were. *#NGB #Assessment*

Don't be consumed, all of you at once, due to his poor eating habits that lack discipline. *No green beans!* Remember, ladies, you are an experience, not an event. You shouldn't be able to be consumed in one setting. There are levels, dimensions, and depths to who you are; however, **you** must take the time to discover it. Then, and only then, will you be able to extend it to others. *#NGB #Theultimate5courseexperience*

Course Two

The Soup

No Green Beans

Chapter 4
What Type of Experience are You?

The "7-Women-to-Every-Man" Myth

When engaged in dialogue regarding relationships, the notorious "7-women-to-1-man" concept always, always, always surfaces. When it does, the dialogue arises to seemingly support that men cheat and/or are emotionally unavailable because… Well, let's be honest—there are a multitude of us, and (to add insult to injury) we are packaged in different shapes, sizes, colors, ethnicities, personalities, etc. …and let's not get into the intricate details of our eyes, lips, hair … our walk, our voice, our touch, our femininity and poise…OUR EXPERIENCE! Our kings and priests are like kids in a candy shop—in their VAST visual imaginations—thinking, "I can't make up my mind….I like that…let me try that…gotta have that…want that, that, that, that and that!!" *(lol)*

While there may be 7 (maybe more) women to every man, I don't believe it puts women (of value) at a disadvantage, especially when the comparables vary in so many ways. It certainly depends on the "type of experience" that you are, which I like to translate to your "code of ethics," a guide of principles designed for those with honesty and integrity. While there may be more "men" than women, the million-dollar question is "How compatible are the ratios: do they hold the same values, morals, standards, goals, etc.?"

When you think of restaurants, what comes to mind? There are lots and lots of restaurants, such as Ruth's Chris, Morton's The

Steakhouse, Cracker Barrel, Olive Garden, Del Frisco's and, yes, even McDonald's. Let's discover the various "types" of restaurants and how they are defined.

Restaurant Chain

A restaurant chain is described as a set of related restaurants in many different locations that are either corporately owned or have franchising available.

Gems, a woman of worth doesn't spread herself all over like a restaurant chain—where you're owned by many, where one can cross state lines and locate you at the next rest stop. You shouldn't be set up as a franchise, where anyone who has the funds to purchase you can; there's no individuality or quality of who you are because your "branded" under someone else. Precious jewels, you are a commodity, a rarity. Show up as an exclusive and not "one of many."

Drive Thru

As previously stated, McDonald's is considered a restaurant. The drive thru that accompanies McDonald's generally accommodates those desiring "fast food," where the purpose is to get something quick and easy when you either don't have time for anything else or you don't feel like the preparation that a nutritious home cooked meal will yield—not to mention, it will more than likely be consumed "on the go." The drive thru is also known to remain open even when the dining room has closed, sometimes as late as 2am or up to 24 hours.

Gems, please don't allow yourself to be treated as a drive thru service, where you're open all times of the night for consumers to get something quick and easy with no intention of staying. Customers frequent late drive thru, oftentimes, because their "preferred" (or everything else) is closed: it's the last resort. I admonish you, precious jewel: please don't find yourself open 24 hours to be consumed at will. Please ensure you aren't being treated as a last resort because you're the only thing open; that's different from being preferred. This also includes "situationships," which has been coined to mean something that's complicated with no direction, defined goal, or status.

Curbside Pick-up

The recent trend towards curbside pick-up has even fine dining restaurants that are known for their elevated experiences to catch the buzz and come aboard. Curbside pick-up allows the comfortability and accommodation of waiting in your vehicle while the restaurant staff brings your order to you, which saves the hassle of physically coming into the restaurant and waiting. While it may seem accommodating enough to include our desired and favorite places (like Capital Grille, Fogo de Chão Brazilian Steakhouse and Bone Fish Grille to name a few), curbside pickup can actually be paralleled with the drive thru experience; however, because it's generally upscale restaurants and the staff are more accommodating in actually bringing the meal out to you, we don't really view it as "cheap" as McDonald's.

Well, my beautiful jewel, it's the same concept. While you may not be open until 2am like the drive thru at McDonald's and your meal may be more palatable to the taste buds than processed chicken nuggets, it could still be considered as "validated" compromise of value. My loves, many times we justify our lower self, communicating "lack of value" because of the "lavishness" that accompanies. If it's obvious that the foundation and totality of a relationship ("situationship") is merely sexual but includes exquisite trips, frequented 5-star restaurants, shopping sprees, and the finest of everything, it's not considered a compromise to your value; however, gem, it is. You're availing yourself to a "side of green beans," but because it's packaged differently, it's okay. My precious jewel, it's not okay. There shouldn't be a price tag associated with who you are. Yes, my love, you are not just costly but <u>priceless</u>. #Nogreenbeans #NGB #Ultimate5courseexperience

All You Can Eat Buffet

A buffet is a process of serving meals in which a variety of dishes are placed in a public area, where guests serve themselves. For those that are familiar with event and meal planning, the cost of a buffet is less expensive than a sit-down dinner. Why? Because the level of accommodation is different and minimal. For a sit-down dinner, waitstaff is needed, and the dinner is normally a full-course experience. On the contrary, with a buffet you simply go and get what you want, which is most of the time a pre-set menu.

Please don't allow yourself to be treated as an all you can eat buffet, where you're discounted with coupons, frequented by many, picked over, and positioned to allow men to take whatever part of you they have a taste for and leave the rest.

Queens, I admonish you; please don't allow yourself to be treated as an all you can eat buffet, where you're discounted with coupons, frequenfounted by many, picked over, and positioned to allow men to take whatever part of you they have a taste for and leave the rest. Oftentimes, the rest of you that they've discarded is the best of you! *#NGB #Nogreenbeans #Theultimate5courseexperience*

The Café

A Café is defined as small restaurant selling light meals, such as sandwiches, wraps, snacks, and drinks.

My beloved jewel, please don't allow yourself to be handled and pursued as "casual." In fact, men don't pursue women they view as casual. If a kingly priest is interested in all of you, then his desire is to make you his, not see you casually (occasionally). Men that are "foodies" have various casual women because (remember) they are absorbed in the "lifestyle of the variety." It's easy for men to fall into the pattern of casual dating; in fact, it's intentional on their part. As we've discussed in our "Wonderful World of Cuisine" chapter, some don't desire a committed relationship, but rather, the ability to consume different types of cuisine at will and on impulse.

Precious jewel, please don't allow yourself to be available on a casual or occasional basis. I admonish you to do introspection with full transparency, authenticity, and vulnerability. Ask yourself if you desire something of more depth than a causal connection but settle for it because, after all, something is better than nothing, right? *Wrong!* You see him casually … you have casual drinks … you have casual fun … you go on casual trips … you have casual sex … and that's the summary: the "situationship" – a casual/ occasional one. My love, women of value don't allow themselves to be treated casually.

Again, if you like it then I love it; however, our pre-requisite for this writing and journey is for us, as gems and jewels, to discover or rediscover our value and ultimately get the depth that we desire and deserve out of relationships. Therefore, we respectfully decline to engage in anything casual, except our attire when necessary ☺.

Fine Dining & Private Dining

This act of fine and private dining *(my favorite)* is an increasingly popular way to have exclusivity or to celebrate an event. Oftentimes, you can tailor private dining rooms or event spaces from cuisine to the room décor to fit your design and needs, depending on the occasion. One reason private dining is my preference is because I absolutely love quiet, intimate, cozy restaurants. The space is reserved, exclusive, intimate, and awaits your arrival. Although private and fine dining may have an additional expense or meal cost requirement, it's worth it; those that request private dining understand the importance thereof.

Jewels, there is importance, necessity, and a lot to be said in a man "preparing" for you. It simply means that he's given thought and preparation to his desire to please, impress, date, and accommodate you. Remember, gems, we are committed to assessment of ourselves and what surrounds us. We just discussed "validated compromise," which is still a form of "green beans": we've compromised simply because the price was right. Pay attention and assess.

I know, gems, when we dialogue about "dating" in our current era, it's obvious that these types of gentlemen are few and far between… but guess what, my love? So are you! You are just as much a rarity— You, the "Ultimate 5-Course Experience" — the woman who has the ability to intrigue a man's intellect and assist with the emergence of his emotions — the woman that brings dimensional value —the woman that has the ability to create an incomparable current in a man's environment that is exhilarating, feminine, sensual, disciplined, and non-sexual (before necessary) — the woman whose foundational value causes her to be exclusive preferred, pursued, and captured.

The Ultimate Experience

From cocktails and wines to elegant entrees, you can feel the opulence with your customized menu options, appreciate truly inspired dishes and drinks that bring elevation, sophistication, and timelessness to your setting. The maître d' is zealous to serve! *I love, love, love elevated dining experiences!* One primary reason is that I love hospitality and accommodations on all levels.

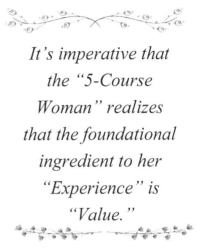

It's imperative that the "5-Course Woman" realizes that the foundational ingredient to her "Experience" is "Value."

While there are many restaurants, there are also many "Experiences." Let's use as an example "The Bygone," an exquisite, elevated dining experience that is located atop the Four Seasons Hotel in Baltimore's Inner Harbor. There is *only one (1)* Bygone Restaurant… *PERIOD* — not different locations in different states — but *One (1)* Bygone Restaurant.

My world class ladies, I challenge you to discover and embrace your dimensional values that create the "Ultimate 5-Course Experience": ambience and qualities that make you not a "one-in-a-million" but a "once-in-a-lifetime" woman. When you know your value, you show up exquisitely and exclusively and have him thinking, "Man, I've had a cut of steak before but never quite like this." *(wink)*

It's imperative that the "5-Course Woman" realizes that the foundational ingredient to her "Experience" is "Value." Your "experience" is what others encounter in your presence. It's who you are: your temperament … your intelligentsia … your ability to ask questions … your ability to stimulate not only sexually but mentally. And if you want to trigger a man's "Love Jones," you must be able to stimulate him emotionally, which isn't—and I repeat isn't—through sex.

Precious jewels, if your sexual prowess (power) is your primary attraction, then I offer my apologies. It's highly unlikely that you will ever have any other part of him: not because you're not valuable but because you've yet to discover your value in the totality of who you are. Sexual prowess alone is a "side of green beans." *#Nogreenbeans #Theultimate5courseexperience*

My Loves, the harsh (bitter) reality is that although our mantras as women are "Girls Rock ... Girl Boss ... Girl Power ... Girl CEO ... Who runs the world? GIRLS!" (and these are true), we will ALWAYS outnumber and outwit men... *END OF STORY*. I don't mean "outwit" to be translated into being manipulative, selfish, and conniving, which are all projections of a lack of quality and low value as a woman. I'm speaking of the incomparable, indescribable, unsurpassed "wit" translated to "value" of a woman that compliments and adds value to a man's life.

Gems, we don't add value to ourselves nor our kings and priests when we are partakers of knowingly sharing men, allowing ourselves to be blatantly disrespected, and accepting the disrespect because it is followed with gifts, trips, verbal manipulations, and in some cases "make up" sex. My love, it's not okay. It's a veil of delusion and deception that prevents you from discovering your value and that ignores the fact that he's a repeat offender ("foodie"); it won't be long until he strikes again. Why? Because the behavior is continually allowed. We previously discussed that men are wired for action. So, if there's no consequence that he can see and feel, such as your removing your presence, he'll continue.

My world-class women, allow me to reiterate as I did in my introduction to you and throughout, our dialogue is NOT about degrading men; it's about what we, as women, tolerate. The million-dollar question is, "Why do we tolerate it?" I'm inclined to believe that it's because we've yet to discover or rediscover our value or the belief that when presented to a man, he will extend the same value!

During my extensive research surrounding dining experiences, I've concluded an intriguing fact. Many fine dining restaurants are small in occupancy with intimate spacing but boast unsurpassed quality, from service to the elevated dining experience. What am I saying? My beautiful jewels, let's not get caught up in "the Majority rules," meaning "Oh well, there are more women than there are men, so I guess I have to take what I can get out here!" Wrong! *#NGB*

The woman who is aware that she's the "Ultimate 5-Course Experience" is resolved with what she possesses and would prefer quality rather than quantity. In other words, she may have men walk away; her dates may be few and far between for 2 reasons. The first is that a woman of value is far past "meal-dating;" she understands her time is valuable and would not use a man for something as shallow as a meal when the man's company isn't her preference. The second reason is that although many will pursue or apply for the position, they are weeded out due by the process and value system she has in place to eliminate what's not preferred. As a result, she attracts and keeps the attention of men of standard who desire, pursue, and capture women of value! *#Nogreenbeans #Theultimate5courseexperience*

52 ❧ *No Green Beans*

Chapter 5

The Wonderful World of Cuisine

"Beware of the Foodie"

food·ie

/ˈfo͞odē/

noun

> *a person with a particular interest in food; a gourmet*

Wikipedia describes a "Food Connoisseur" as a specialist who has an ardent (passionate, enthusiastic) or refined (advanced, superior) interest in food and who eats food not only out of hunger but due to their interest or hobby. A foodie is primarily a person who <u>loves</u> and <u>lives</u> to try different restaurants and cuisines. According to *Science Today*, the average person has about **10,000 taste buds,** and they're replaced every 2 weeks or so. The palates (taste buds) of foodies enjoy "a variety" of cuisine. No matter how superior the restaurant is and/or how unsurpassed the cuisine is, they will <u>always</u> frequent other restaurants—simply because it's what they do. Their delight is in the "difference."

Jewels, we are a world of cuisine—take your pick: light, dark, brown, caramel…brown eyes, blue eyes…thin frame, medium frame, curvy frame. We encompass Soul Food, Thai, Greek, Chinese, Indian,

Vietnamese, French, Mexican, Italian, Caribbean, Spanish, Middle Eastern, Brazilian, African, and a host of other cuisines. Yes, we are arrayed in different shapes, sizes, colors, and we were "created" to satisfy the palate of every part of a man in every way.

Ladies, Ladies, Ladies! Please, I beg of you, don't find yourself entangled with someone who doesn't see your value as pronounced and exclusive as it is. It doesn't matter how much of a delicacy (delightful, pleasing) you are; some men will never see you as their "one and only," but rather their "one of their <u>many</u>" favorite places to frequent and dine.

Gems, the harsh yet exhilarating reality is that some men are simply <u>not</u> ready. It goes beyond who you are as a woman… It goes beyond the royal care you give him…. It goes beyond how you hold him down…. It goes beyond how loyal you are … and yes, my love, it certainly goes beyond how you perform in the bedroom. The truth is: He's just not ready, and if we're honest, he's displayed it time and time and time and time again.

It doesn't matter how much of a delicacy (delightful, pleasing) you are; some men will never see you as their "one and only," but rather their "one of their <u>many</u>" places to frequent and dine.

Remember, jewels, when we speak of valuing ourselves, it empowers us; it gives us necessary awareness that translates to "I will not allow myself to be mishandled in any way." Jewels, if your love and loyalty are indebted to someone who doesn't see your value, then it's not the man who's at fault, my love—it's you. How can you assess if someone doesn't see your value? They mishandle you, take you for granted, treat you as an option and not a priority.

However, I must give you the challenging but liberating truth: He will never see your value if you don't see it first and value yourself. Remember, people can only do what we allow them to do. At this point, our million-dollar questions should be, "How do I discover my value?" and "What is it that I need to address internally that prevents me from doing so?"

One of the most deceiving, self-sabotaging thoughts that we (women) can have is thinking we can change or attempt to change a man—thinking such as "He's never had anyone like me" … "Wait until I get through with him" … "These women don't have anything on me" … "He knows where home is." The question I'd like to propose is while he knows where home is, "How many stops did he make along the way?" or "If he even made it home?"

Queens, please know that "home" is a safe (harmless), sacred (revered, consecrated) place. Not a dysfunctional "home plate" like in baseball, where the player begins at home but must go around the field and touch 3 other bases before he returns to the home plate—only to do it over again. Home shouldn't be his "#1 in a pool of 3." Home shouldn't be where he is for holidays; home shouldn't be his "main lady" when he has seconds and thirds—and all three know of each other.

Sweetheart, your worth goes far beyond that. Although you may "love" him, when loving him is harming you, it's no longer love; it's toxicity, dysfunction, and trauma. *[We discuss this in detail in the chapter "Call the Paramedics, I have food poisoning."]* #NoGreenBeans #NGB

I suggest as women that we should be a more reserved with our vulnerabilities, boundaries, and assessments with men. Not playing games, but rather to ensure that the man can handle the capacity of who we are. Queens, the prerequisite to this is that <u>you</u> must know your capacity, value, and worth.

Oftentimes, we don't <u>see</u> what men are saying because we are listening and <u>not</u> watching. We perceive his words to align with what we <u>want</u> them to mean instead of what he <u>displays</u>. He can tell you for months or even years that he wants to be with you and only you, that he's leaving his girlfriend/wife, yet his actions boldly state something totally different. His actions translate to, "Let me tell her what's necessary to keep her close because I want to be able to have Italian cuisine *(you)* when I feel like having Italian cuisine *(you)*...although I had Mediterranean *(someone else)* just last night." My gems, it sounds like he needs a palate cleanser ☺.

When assessing the capacity of another, we must realize that acting on impulse (thought, urge, feeling) doesn't equate to him showing readiness for your 5-course experience. In fact, impulse denotes a lack of discipline. When we act on impulse, it's based upon feeling and compulsion (pressure, force). His impulse (desire, instinct, urge) is based upon "when he thinks of you." Is it when he's bored? ... Is it when he desires your sexual experience? ... Or is it because he genuinely enjoys your company and likes you as a person?

Ladies, you **<u>do</u>** know that a man can be mesmerized (fascinated) with the experience you provide and not really be into you, don't you? Therefore, you only hear from him when he has a taste for "Italian" and because you're always open, serving even when dinner is over, food is put away, and the kitchen is cleaned and "should be" closed. You proceed to take the green beans out of the freezer, put them in the microwave, and serve them.

Sweetheart, you're worth much more! But I'm not speaking of you, precious gem, maybe someone you know…*(wink)* someone you know!

Impulse and compulsion are a couple of reasons why men can pay for sexual encounters and never see someone again or have casual, repeated encounters with the same person and never be connected emotionally *(see The Ultimate Synergy chapter)*. They can frequent gentlemen's clubs and request the same women each time because men are about an "experience," a journey.

However, my precious jewels, they also enjoy the challenge of not being able to figure someone out. I have several platonic male friends, and you'd be surprised how they view women with (what they refer to as) "no standard." I've heard them say, "I really liked her, but she slept with me too soon" … "She was too loose" … "I could have got it if I wanted it."

Of course, the men may have followed suit but, ladies, to reiterate (repeat), "Men follow our lead." It's up to us to separate ourselves from the rest and present ourselves as women of value. It's disheartening that men now turn down sex because women practically stalk men to throw themselves sexually. That tells me in some form or another, sex is underrated, and men are screaming for us to offer something else. Don't get me wrong…they will take *it (well some will)*, but they really desire so much more. My love, what's necessary has be to be ignited in him to get a different response. *#NoGreenBeans #NGB #Theultimate5courseexperience*

Gems let's not forget that food connoisseurs are defined as experts and specialists (professionals) in their industries. They have a strategy for food tasting; they have a strategy for how to consume large volumes and stay with a figure. What does this mean? Men that are foodies all have a common goal: to consume! They are intentional and strategic ... they are smooth talkers ... they are charmers; some are very generous ... some are manipulators ... Or maybe not—maybe they are honest that all they want to do is hook up.

They are labeled as experts and specialists based upon their continued and successful reviews. They have little to no intention of making you anything more than a dish in their world of cuisine. This has nothing to do with you; they've not matured to the place of discipline and more than likely have no desire to be disciplined. They deliberately test you to see where you are and if it's allowed.

Ladies let's put a pin right here for a moment.... Yes, men will "test" you. They want to see what type of woman you are, which determines the category they place you in. So, "show up," my love, as the unforgettable, irreplaceable gem that you are.

When we, as women, compete about who's better in bed, well, my incomparable queens, we are in trouble because we're worth so much more than a sexual encounter.

Let's say you have interest in him, but you get the feeling that he only wants one thing. What gives you that feeling? Is it because that's the subject when you all hook up? Is it because he only contacts you when he wants to come over (or vice versa) but never plans or initiates a date? *(Oh, and out only to get drinks doesn't count.)* Sweetheart, is it because you gave in too soon and trained his palate sexually before you did mentally, spiritually, and/or emotionally? Be honest, gem, because being true to self is the only way transformational healing can take place.

It's in this moment that we face the bitter, shameful, twisted truth, when your text (or sext) thread is longer than the one phone call, Face Time, or visit. (*Ladies… explicit Face Timing doesn't count.*) You've stimulated nothing but his organs. When we, as women, compete about who's better in bed, well, my incomparable queens, we are in trouble because we're worth so much more than a sexual encounter. Not only that, but the real "tea" is that the man loves when women compete because he gets to have the best of both—all three, or even all four—worlds.

Next course of action? We generally take our frustrations, hurt, shame, and pain from **_his_** behavior out on each other. We call and harass each other, fight each other, dishonor each other when in reality, it wasn't the other woman's fault *(well, not all the time)*—rather, the man's. Remember, the food connoisseur's desire, goal, and purpose are to sample and frequent different cuisine. Come on, my loves… *#Nogreenbeans*

Ladies, have you ever felt betrayed…heartbroken…used… not good enough…bewildered…etc.? Have you experienced being mishandled in any way, whether sharing a man without your consent, becoming a victim of domestic abuse, being called out of your name or being disrespected in any capacity? During those times, did you ever ask yourself, "What's wrong with me? Why am I not good enough?"

I think the best of us have; I know I can attest that I certainly have. I've questioned my competence, my esteem, my value as a woman. Although immature at the time, I compared myself to other women, desperately wanting to know what they had that I didn't. My comparison quickly became envy and then anger. I was angry, hurt, and frustrated because I deeply desired a part of him that he either didn't want to give or did not have the capacity to give. I couldn't understand how my loyalty could be betrayed because, after all, I would <u>never</u> think of doing such a thing.

Then, as I began to grow, learn, discover my value…grow, learn, discover my value…grow and learn… I realized that there wasn't anything wrong with me. Rather, it was the lack of process and/or maturity on the man's part. As stated previously, and I reiterate, jewels, some men just aren't ready. *#Period* However, we try and "make" them ready by placing unrealistic goals on them and unrealistic expectations on ourselves, by saying things like "I can get him to change his mind and want me and only me." My precious beloved jewel, that will never happen until he is ready for it to happen…and guess what? The bitter, harsh reality is that sometimes, gems—just sometimes—we are preparing men for other women, other relationships, and other families.

I know, I know, I know … it makes some of us cringe, especially after all you've invested, but it's the truth. Sometimes, when our kings and priests "get it," it's too late. Why does it "click" for them when you're fed up and have moved on? Jewels, men are hard-wired for action, not lip service. That's why, sometimes, it's not until they come home and either the home is completely cleared out or the women has departed that they "feel" it. That's why he really doesn't fight tooth and nail to get you back until you've *"taken action"* and stopped all communication, which is a verb (action word) not mere lip service.

Let's also beware of him doing what it takes to get you back; this doesn't always mean that he really loves you and desires to make you his only. Oftentimes, that can be translated to, "I will do what I have to do to keep you close so that I can continue to have my 'Italian' night when I feel like it."

Some behaviors of the food connoisseur are paralleled with the Narcissistic personality; traits include patterns of self-centeredness, arrogant thinking and **behavior**, a lack of empathy and consideration for other people, and an excessive need for admiration. Others often describe these individuals as cocky, manipulative, selfish, patronizing, and demanding.

My incomparable jewels, you are worth so much more than an option. You're the ultimate exclusive. *(wink)* #NoGreenBeans #Theultimate5courseexperience #NGB

No Green Beans

Chapter 6
Call the Paramedics — I have Food Poisoning

(Toxic Relationships)

tox·ic

/ˈtäksik/

> *Poisonous, venomous, dangerous, destructive harmful, unsafe, fatal, deadly, lethal*

Food poisoning (also called foodborne illness) is illness caused by eating contaminated, spoiled, or toxic food. Infectious organisms—including **bacteria**, viruses, and parasites or their toxins—are the most common causes of food poisoning. As we know, there are good and bad bacteria. Untreated bacteria can lead to other diseases and complications. A parasite is an organism that lives in or on an organism of another species (its host) and benefits by deriving nutrients at the other's expense.

Now that we've reviewed various ways that food contamination can affect us in our physical bodies, I'd like to metaphorically compare how it relates to contaminates in relationships. When toxins and dysfunctions are ingested into our hearts and souls, it's like we are intaking poison. Whether the toxins are derived from our childhood, contributing to how we love and receive love, or be it from dysfunctional people we allow in our lives who spew and inject us with toxins, both contribute to how we are positioned in relationships, either nutritional or poisonous.

My beautiful gems, as you are aware by now, we discussed in depth the importance of self-awareness and assessment. It's critical that we evaluate while collecting data (dating) and/or prior to entering a serious relationship. Oftentimes, the reservations are there—either we feel and or see them— however, we ignore them; we are so zealous and emotionally led that we justify the relationship because it's something that we desire. My loves let's not create a fantasy: take it for what it is!

I can remember a time when I was dating a gentleman, and we had a peculiar connection that mutually attracted us. As time progressed, I (through assessment) began to realize that although we were equally attracted and both single, we were in different places of "singleness." I had been single for some time, had healed, and was in a position to give and to receive. He, on the other hand, was just emerging from a sustained relationship. Although we vibed in every way, we were in two different places—I knew that. It was nothing he did but rather something I "assessed." Although there was interest, I knew he couldn't provide what I desired (long term) because (1) he didn't have it to give and (2) he didn't want it. It wasn't that he didn't want me, but he was exhaling, and I was ready to inhale. Nothing wrong…just two different places.

No, my loves, I didn't try to "make it work" ... I didn't self-deceive myself and think, "Let me see where this goes" ... I didn't try to "change his mind." I took it for what it was and not what I "wanted" it to be; I took the "sting" and broke it off at that juncture, rather than risk the chance of getting "wounded" and needing open heart surgery later. Gems remember to guard your heart for out of it flows the issues of life ☺.

There are things we must be able to detect and assess early on and use preventive measures (and not react "as a result of") as these things can become toxic situations.

We've discussed the "It's complicated" relationship. (*I'm still waiting for someone to explain to me what that is without justifying its toxicity...period.*) If something can't be clearly defined, then it lacks purpose. Everything we do should have a purpose for it. Every organization should have a mission statement that explains why it (you) exist.

"How do toxic relationships begin?" some may ask. Toxicity can be both foundational and developmental. My loves, if we have limited to no knowledge of our value, then we are breeding grounds for toxicity. Why? Because our lack of value translates to so many things in relationships, related to how we handle ourselves and how we allow ourselves to be handled.

Our traits, thoughts, and behaviors are contaminated. What does that mean? It means that somewhere on this journey called life, we were susceptible to and consumed contaminates. My loves, if our souls are contaminated (toxic), it affects us in various ways; we have damaged emotions, marred souls, and scared hearts. As a result, we attract toxic men that ultimately solidify the toxic relationships because... *What makes up a relationship? People, right? Of course.* A relationship is only as strong, mature, solid, supportive, weak, toxic, and selfish as the participants "in" the relationship. We oftentimes treat our relationships as if they are a separate entity and that "we" aren't a part of them.

Either toxicity will cause us to speak words to others that cut to the core or our toxicity will silence our voice because we inwardly don't believe anything we have to say is of value or importance. Toxicity will draw "Daddyless" daughters to "Motherless" sons. Toxicity will justify the cause to be in a relationship with a married man (with a family) for years on end and be satisfied for a piece of him and his time.

Contaminates (toxins) in our soul will justify 2-3 women knowingly sharing a man because he provides financially for everyone. A virus (also a form of toxicity) will justify consistent inconsistency from men because of their bedroom game. Toxins in our soul will search for love in sex and fall in love with someone on a sexual foundation, who has never offered a date beyond drinks and/or "Netflix and chill."

Jewels, again, I sincerely admonish you to please get healed from the underlying challenges that cause toxins in us so that your perspective of men—what you desire and deserve—isn't jaded. When we have toxins in our system, it affects our vision and how we view and assess things. In fact, when we are contaminated, the toxins and dysfunctions take on a personality of their own and do the choosing for us! So now, we aren't choosing prospective partners, but rather dysfunction is choosing dynamic disasters. When we are healed holistically, we aren't seeing through a dysfunctional lens, but from a healthy, balanced space that yields results.

Contaminates (toxins) in our soul will justify 2-3 women knowingly sharing a man because he provides financially for everyone.

My jewels, when our perspectives are jaded, it's challenging to see men who aren't the best for us—meaning those that are toxic look the best to us because we view them from a toxic place. Yes, jewels, we are committed to our own personal development, but can I tell you? ... Our kings and priests have challenges as well. They too carry pain (past and present), rejections, insecurities, and fear, except they carry, and process differently than we do.

These areas often contribute to the toxicity of emotionally unavailable men. Areas that I've discussed with other women and have personally encountered are issues like pain, defeat, unforgiveness, gambling, pornography, financial challenges, heartbreak, abandonment from mother or father or both, and sexual abuse (molestation, prison rape). Just as we discussed in our pre-requisite about trauma and how it affects our balanced, healthy, holistic growth, it's the same with men, except they become emotionally unavailable.

Ladies, are we able to identify if a man is emotionally unavailable and how it can eventually materialize into toxicity in relationships? Some ways are a lack of communication; it's challenging for him to not only express how he feels about you but even to have an intellectual conversation. He's more alive when drinking or engaging sexually.

When our kings and priests are emotionally unavailable, rest assured, something or someone has their emotions. It could be that the last time he opened his heart, he got hurt. Gems, contrary to what we believe, men love just as hard (if not harder) than we do. Therefore, it's so important for us to do an assessment and decide based upon the findings.

I remember dating this guy for a short period of time; he was an entrepreneur, so his schedule was rigorous. I, too, was building, so we were aligned in that aspect. I started to notice when we would have discussions about vulnerability, intimacy, matters of the heart, etc., there was a brick wall. We could discuss building, sports, children all day, but again, he was extremely blocked off in certain areas. I learned that he was recently divorced after being married almost half of his life (20 years) ...but guess what, my loves? He didn't know that he didn't have anything to give. In my heart of hearts, I really believe that he wanted to move past where he was; I believed that he really had an interest, but he just couldn't—it was too much.

My jewels, it was my responsibility to assess and decide. Should I continue to date one-fourth of him? Nope, it wasn't even half of him. Ladies, we must take the time to assess and not desire a man or relationship so badly that we're willing to take anything, even if it's a portion of him. #Nogreenbeans

My loves, are you able to assess if a man is violent, a narcissist, a manipulator, an addict (drugs, alcohol, sex, work), a controller, or an abuser whether verbal, physical, emotional or financially? If any of my precious gems and jewels reading now have been abused in any way, I apologize; it was not your fault. You didn't deserve it, and you're worth far more than that! It hurts my heart to think of the abuse we suffer, as women: sexual abuse, emotional abuse, verbal abuse, physical abuse, mental abuse, financial abuse, workplace abuse, gender abuse and others!

I know the impact this topic may have and, my love, I took the chance anyway because I live on the premise of "discovering the courage to conquer"— face painful, shameful, truths that will ultimately liberate if dealt with. This is why, I consulted and partnered with a licensed mental health professional with this project because, my loves, healing is not only needed, but it's necessary.

I can remember, as if it were yesterday, various times in my journey and process where I had to muster the courage to face what intended to plague me and keep me in emotional bars. At times, it seemed easier to ignore, suppress and use fillers, which are people, places, and things to fill emptiness and voided areas; however, my areas of brokenness were pronounced in different areas to include relationships and my choice of men.

One of my favorite songs in the 90's was "Secret Lovers" by Atlantic Starr, I loooved the rhythm, hooks, and runs. In this song, two people were clearly having an extramarital affair, and they both enjoyed it—making mention and asking the question, if committing adultery is so wrong then why does it feel so right? I mean, who wants to hide the fact that they love someone? When you love someone, you don't care who knows, right? As a matter of fact, you want everyone to know!

My loves, may I pause here for a moment? If you are a secret, then I strongly admonish you to reconsider if you have a relationship. You are a woman of value and a woman of worth. If you are good enough to be seen in private, you are good enough to be seen in public. My loves, I'm speaking of when we sometimes move too fast with a man and now that you've maybe slept with him too soon—or misappropriated the two you hanging out and talking—you "assume" he's your man... not so.

May I also suggest, just because you spend time together doesn't mean you aren't a "secret."

Men don't think like we do. Remember, that's why it's critical to allow the man to drive the car, and <u>you</u> decide if you like where he's taking you; if not, my love, exit the car. Gems, we are taking responsibility and actions for our own lives, time and space. *#NGB*

May I also suggest, just because you spend time together doesn't mean you aren't a "secret." Okay, my love, take these examples for free: If he knows your neighbors, dog, and almost your entire family and you only know his 3 friends... *my love, think again....* If he is always at your place and you are rarely or never invited to his place… *my love, think again* … If you're doing all the planning for dates and all the initiating for spending time… *my love, think again* … If you've never been invited to meet his immediate family (parents, siblings, aunties, uncles), especially for holidays and events … *my love, think again.*

Men are skilled and successful at making a woman feel like they are the only one when they're <u>with</u> them, and guess what? You are the only one but so are the others (in some instances)!

I can remember when I was in my early twenties and had fallen in love with this guy; he was a bit older than I was, and we were inseparable. We spent most days and nights together. We went out. He spoiled me like crazy. He introduced me to just about everyone he could. I was known as his "lady." So, when we were together, it was us—we dominated.

One sunny day after about 2 years of dating, he had just returned from having my car (that he'd purchased for me) serviced. He dropped it off, got into his car, and pulled off. I hopped in my car, started the ignition, and pulled down the mirrored sun visor to apply lip gloss… when suddenly, several utility and other bill receipts (in a woman's name) fell into my lap. I attempted to call the telephone number that was listed on the receipts—after all, this was my man, and I wanted to know who she was. The phone rang … "Hello," said the woman on the other end…. I said, "Hello," introduced myself, and explained the reason for my call, including asking her if she knows ******. I then found out that she was his "live-in" girlfriend and was expecting a set of twins in a few months.

I was too much in shock to be upset. The only question I could ask was, "How could this be when we spent so much time together?" not to mention how close we were. By this time, I was already in love with him and had no intention on breaking it off—after all, I considered him "my" man, and she was the trespasser...although they lived together and she was pregnant with his children.

My loves, I shared this experience because I understand how sometimes you're in too deep and so is the man. Many have asked me if I think it's possible for someone to be torn between two people, and my answer is "absolutely." However, I do feel with men, it's for different reasons. They may have a woman that they consider their "lady" and defined as such, they may have a "buddy," one they can chill and be themselves with, they may have one that is experimental in the bedroom, they may have one because she's a source of peace and comfort, and they may have a lady that's loyal to them but doesn't hold them accountable because she feels that she should love him at any cost and be down for "whatever". *My love, that's incorrect.*

A healthy connection has boundaries. Someone who really cares for you and understands what that means wouldn't suggest that hurting you (in any capacity) is that same as caring for you unconditionally. My loves, we should never be in too deep where we will do "anything" for someone. When "helping you" is "harming me," that's not love its toxicity.

Remember, we are women of value with standards, and because we have a commitment to our personal growth and to discover our value, I would gladly say that there is nothing about that 21-year-old girl that I would consider doing now. As I disclosed before, my value had to be discovered and has emerged over the course of time.

"So, which is easier," some may ask, "to continue or to break it off?" Well, I'll be the first to agree that nothing is easy about pain, betrayal, and heartbreak, while still loving someone. Although it may be easier to stay and remain in the "situationship," this thought process and behavior will result in a toxic relationship because now both women (in some cases 3) have subconsciously agreed to share the man. Furthermore, it's only easier because we refuse go through the process that making wise, healthy decisions will yield. So, in essence, it may seem easier just to "stay," but long-term it causes greater damage to you emotionally and mentally and to your value system, which is hidden and buried.

It's toxic when we, ladies, are with men because our biological time clocks are ticking. It's toxic when we are mishandled and mistreated in <u>any</u> capacity and continue with someone. It's toxic when we justify because we have children involved. A thought to ponder for my precious gems to which it may apply is, "If you're in a toxic relationship with your child's father, what do you think the child is learning and observing when the parents are together?" Toxicity, right? Does this give the child a healthy perception of love or does it teach them that contamination is love?

We've discussed what causes our kings and priests to become contaminated, how to identify it, and how it affects us… but, my loves, what happens when <u>we</u> are contaminated, poisonous, and toxic? What happens when <u>we</u> sabotage every good thing? What happens when <u>we</u> never feel good enough? What happens when <u>we</u> must test his devotion by starting arguments and being crafty for a response (because that's your history)? What happens when we are victims of "Vicarious Trauma," which happens when we embody everyone else's trauma and toxicity, and as a result, it affects us in pronounced ways?

My loves, we can become targets for vicarious trauma when we have unresolved pain because it subconsciously attracts the same. We can also become targets for vicarious trauma because we are "loyal" to a fault with no boundaries (which we discussed previously). My loves,

I reiterate, if loyalty must be tested and proven by someone's repeated cycles of mishandling, misusing, and/or abusing you, that's not loyalty: it's manipulation, dysfunction, and toxicity.

Jewels, what is a man absorbing and feasting upon when he's in your presence? When he partakes from your table, does it nourish him, or does it make him sick with contaminations, requiring medical attention? There are several nutritional aspects that should be inclusive of your "Ultimate 5-Course Experience."

You should be pleasing to the eye. My loves, this is the importance of self-care, not merely keeping up with yourself to keep a man; self-care is rooted in self-love. Before he knows anything about how you taste—which are your attributes, character, etc.—he should be able to look and say, "Hmm...that looks delicious; I think I'll try that." Remember, ladies, men are visual. Be appealing in your own way and fall in love with yourself and all of your imperfections. *I know I have!* You are not meant to resemble any other women in height, build, weight, or any other attribute that makes you exclusive! Let's not compare ourselves, gems; remember, we are incomparable *(hugs)*.

Next, you should be tasteful to his palate. By this place in our journey, you should know, precious gem, that I'm speaking in a non-sexual way. When he encounters you, when he draws from a place in you, is he drawing from a fresh, clean, pure stream of water that's derived from a holistic place.... Or is he regurgitating due to the contamination and toxicity that he's consumed from you?

I'm certain we have all dealt with toxicity in one form or another; I certainly have. However, we must be in a place where we are able to identify whether we are toxic or whether toxicity is seeking to introduce itself to us. The only way we can differentiate is by seeing through a holistic and healthy lens.

When we operate from a holistic place of healing, then everyone in our sphere of influence benefits thereby. My beautiful gems and jewels, please, please, please take time and courage to heal. It will be the one of the most liberating decisions we will ever make; if not, we will bleed on those that didn't cut us and sabotage every good thing that attempts to get near us. *(Hugs)*

#NoGreenBeans#Theultimate5courseexperience #NGB

The Palate Cleanser

(Intermezzo)

A neutral-flavored food or drink that removes food residue from the tongue allowing one to more accurately assess a new flavor

No Green Beans

Chapter 7
The Ultimate Synergy

(Sexuality v Sensuality)

Alright, my love, we've completed two of our five courses, and if you've noticed, there are still three courses to go—<u>and</u> you're still at the dinner table☺.

If you've followed and implemented what we've discussed up until now, you will have begun the journey to a healthy sense of self, confidence, and discovery/rediscovery of value, which yields the ingredients of an "Ultimate 5-Course Experience." We've discussed our prerequisites, which are self-awareness and inner healing, our dining etiquette and our standards, and have explored various "types" of restaurants and categorized ourselves as such.

It is now time for the ***palate cleanser***. "What is that?" some may ask. The palate cleanser (originated in France and common in French multi course meals) is a neutral-flavored food or drink that removes food residue and lingering flavors from the tongue, which enables one to "accurately" assess the taste of a new flavor. In cultures where diversity of flavors in dishes are custom, the palate cleanser is considered an essential companion to main dishes.

Just as the *palate cleanser* is an essential companion to main dishes, it too is essential to go along with your experience. The purpose for the subtitle "The Ultimate Synergy" is to discuss the crucial place of the experience that we are now in. Sexuality and sensuality must be established, determining factors moving forward. My love, this juncture must be defined, differentiated, and decided. Here, you solidify or sever where you are with a person. This is where sexuality is differentiated from sensuality.

Gems, please allow me to reiterate; this is not merely a book— It's a transformational tool that, if implemented, will compel and propel you to show up as the "Ultimate 5-Course Experience" you were designed to be and that real men desire, pursue, and capture. With that said… there's a systematic approach (a formula) that must be inclusive in the dining experience.

At this point in the course, your experience (who you are), along with the *palate cleanser*, should begin the process of eliminating all the lingering flavors and previous "dishes" that he's consumed prior to you. This is the time when you introduce his appetite to your dimensional experience. At this point, he's had a taste of your beauty, femininity, class, poise, and non-sexual/sensual energy, which now motivates him to desire more of what he's had the "opportunity" to partake in. Yes, I said the "opportunity," as everyone should not have access to you. This, my loves, is our prerequisite, our standard and proper dining etiquette☺. #NGB #theUltimate5courseexperience

Gems, do you know what really compelled me to write this book? I was becoming very disheartened at the way we (precious and valuable jewels) were oversexualized by society and how we presented ourselves the same way (at times).

We've become very unrestricted with our most beautiful, prized possession, so much so that we compare how good we are in bed to the next woman. We equate that to the totality of who we are, and it's **not** the totality of who we are! When we take the time and courage to discover our true value, we will clearly see the beauty that we possess as women that includes all the attributes and nutrients that we have and give—which is faaarrrrr more valuable than sex. My loves, I don't know about you, but I'd rather a man think of me and say how mentally, emotionally, spiritually, financially, physically, and sexually attractive I am—not just minimize my entire "5-course experience" to a sexual encounter ("a side of green beans").

Ladies, men get bored; our kings and priests are built for an experience: a challenge. Let's be honest… think about a guy you've only had a sexual relationship with *(if it applies)*; when you think about it, that was the extent. Whether disguised in trips, shopping, financial stability, etc., the foundation was sexual.

In totality, you my beautiful gem, are an "Ultimate 5-Course Experience!" Please don't allow anyone to minimize you only for sex and don't you minimize yourself and offer only sex! My love, you're worth soooo much more! *(Hugs)* #Nogreenbeans #NGB

Jewels, sexuality is about our sexual feelings, thoughts, attractions, and behaviors towards others. One can find another physically, sexually, or emotionally attractive; they all play a part in our sexuality which is diverse, personal, and is an important part of who we are. Sensuality is the ability to fully experience one's senses. Smelling, tasting, seeing, hearing, touching, and feeling are combined to awaken the body. Sensuality is affected by the level of stimulation. Jewels, our ability to display sensuality with a man is paramount, an essential skill when positioning yourself as the "Ultimate 5-Course Experience."

Being in tune sensually is the ability to communicate in non-sexual, intangible manners that reach and connect in a deeper and different way with men. Developing the skill of sensuality will enable you to show up in the magnetic, lasting attraction rather than in the temporary, shallow sexuality that men can get anywhere—I repeat **anywhere.** *#NGB!*

When engaging someone with whom you have interest, it is then time to pay attention. Watch your actions; don't be too aggressive, especially in sexual suggestions and body language. Be attentive to him in the sense of getting to know ***him***, not his status, influence, or affluence. I'm not minimizing these things, but I'm certainly not maximizing them either.

I believe we gotten extremely materialistic, surface, and shallow when it comes to getting to know someone and dating. This isn't a job interview. I'm a life partner, not an employee; so are you! If I'm getting to know someone, I must be honest and say, "How one treats others is far more important to me that how many figures one has in the bank." One's loyalty and trustworthiness are far more important to me than a stock portfolio.

When getting to know someone, ladies, use your sight to see. Develop the skill and take the time to see past the surface of him: the surface of what he says, the surface of what he has, and the surface of what he portrays. It's only when you exercise the ability to have vision (the big picture) beyond sight (the immediate) that you can make a proper assessment.

Being in tune sensually is the ability to communicate in non-sexual, intangible manners that reach and connect in a deeper and different way with men.

This, my love, isn't operating from a place of low self-esteem, where you are leery of everything, but rather being observant. There's a difference. A gentleman once asked me if

I was guarded, and my response was, "Yes, I am" — not from a place of dysfunction, where I'm comparing him to another, but from a place of awareness of my worth. I am precious cargo with tons of valuables in the home of my being, so I monitor the traffic "around" my home. Likewise, be the dimensional experience that causes him to "see" you in a different light, where he's like "wow" — and the "wow" isn't derived from the place of good sex. *#Nogreenbeans #NGB*

Before we get into "him," we must first discover the sound that we hear about our own worthiness of being loved, valued, and cherished unconditionally. This is critical in determining how you "receive" attraction and love. Your kingly priest may be surrounding your space, but because you don't see yourself as worthy, you may subconsciously sabotage (damage, disrupt).

We must be able to hear him on a "deeper" level. How are we able to do this? Because you are the "Ultimate 5-Course Experience," you must ask questions and present intriguing dialogue that stimulates his mind and causes him to relate from a place other than his genitals. As we've discovered previously, men group all women together initially until the woman separates herself from the rest by her "non-sexual" experience.

Some may ask why I am suggesting "non-sexual" energy and actions. Well, my love, let's be honest… sex is overrated and undervalued. It's undervalued so much that men can go and pay for sex on a corner, they can go into a gentlemen's club and have access to a private room or they can have 2 or more women sexually indulge with them at the same time.

I've completed a survey in the coming chapters from real men with real answers asking what their top 3 needs from their lady were, and you'd be surprised at the answers. You know why, my loves?

Because when a man <u>chooses</u> a woman to be his, there's certain criteria for the woman. Now he may have sex and casuals throughout, but his "Lady" is required to have several things. I've been on both sides and being used as "a side of green beans" doesn't feel good—mentally, spiritually, emotionally or physically.

Let's discuss the "smell" … My loves, the experience that a man encounters when meeting, pursuing, dating, or merely being in your presence should be that of a rarity. You should be a "Wow Factor," a "Breath of Fresh Air," when he encounters the enchanting fragrance of your spirit and the flavor of your soul—not just your face but the crisp, refreshing fragrance of your smile and laughter that emanates from a liberated being.

My jewels, let's put a pin right here… I admonish you… please, please, please heal from previous traumas, disappointments, rejections, and any other pain designed to plague and keep you in emotional prisons.

Since we're talking about men, can I tell you that processed and mature men don't care for women that bring drama and toxicity? A part of the "Ultimate 5-Course Experience" is being an "island of calm (peace) in a world of chaos." It's not picking arguments, being combative, participating in immaturity to "get his attention," stalking his social media, phone, and everything else. My love, you're not getting his attention: you're giving him a headache. Remember, our pre-requisite to the being the "Ultimate 5-Course Experience" is healing from the trauma that oftentimes causes this level of behavior.

Okay, loves… so I hear you saying, "You don't understand what he does to make me act this way." I get it; however, I'd like to reiterate our commitment to self which doesn't blame others but rather takes responsibility for our own actions because that's all we have control of. It may sound harsh, my beautiful gem, but at the end of the day, we're on a transformational journey that requires us to sometimes face bitter, harsh realities, including "One can only do what I allow them to do."

I know, jewels... when we love, we love hard, but may I propose that love first begins with self (our prerequisite). When we discover our value, it translates to "Yes, I may love you, but I love me more." May I also suggest that love is not being mishandled, abused, or disrespected in anyway. I will remove myself first because <u>I will not allow it</u>, and I encourage you not to allow it either. *#Nogreenbeans #Knowyourworth*

"Taste" ... what is the function? Taste depicts... it deciphers ...it separates flavor.

Jewels, what is your "flavor"? Our "flavor" is what we're comprised of: our swag, our attributes, our characteristics, our qualities. When he's had a taste of your non-sexual ingredients, it makes you an exclusive (select, limited, private). Because of your experience, including dimensional capacity, you've introduced him to a dish that (although he's never had it) he enjoys.

At this point, my loves, you can bet your bottom dollar that you've ignited something in him—something he's yet to encounter ... and, ladies, I don't mean a sexual encounter. He's tasted your non-sexual experience, and guess what? He likes it! He's intrigued by your thought process ... he's mesmerized by the beauty of your spirit and soul ... he's smitten by your timeless class ... he's flattered by your femininity ... he's subconsciously becoming magnetically attracted to you because you're presenting something different. Therefore, he's valuing something different. *#NGB*

If the ambience of your being could speak, what would it say? Did you know, gems, that your spirit, soul, and body comprise your ambience, which is your atmosphere, mood, setting, etc.? What environment do you create? No, precious jewel, I'm not speaking of candles, sultry sounds, and lingerie for a sexual encounter. I'm speaking of how a man feels in your presence. Do you ignite the king and priest in him, or do you provoke the pig in him? *[Sidebar: What you ignite in him, my love, is what portion of him you will get.]* Is he enamored not only by your physical beauty, but the beauty of your conversation, confidence, and brilliance? We're speaking of the "Ultimate 5-Course Experience," which is the totality of the finest ingredients of who you are.

Finally, the undeniable attribute of non-sexual intimacy is "touch." Gems, as I know you are aware, intimacy is not sex—contrary to what some men and women believe. There are tons of non-sexual gestures that stimulate other areas in him, like holding hands, cuddling, a massage, a back rub, preparing meals together, working out, visiting amusement parks, doing something he likes, etc. If likes football, girl, get a jersey ... If he likes cars, grab tickets to the auto show ... If he's an entrepreneur, get into his flow. Bring yourself into his world; show him that what's important to him is important to you, even if it's not your ideal.

Remember, true, lasting connections are about being selfless, not selfish. It's not about us all the time; sometimes we can be savages: selfish, spoiled, and bougie *(lol)*. Don't misunderstand... there's nothing wrong with being spoiled. As a matter of fact, both of my hands are raised! But guess what? I'm going to spoil him also. Love is mutual. It's about making adjustments (not to be confused with compromise); there's a difference.

Ladies, when we allow a man to experience us sensually before sexually, it gives us an advantage because his emotional triggers have been awakened, which is his stream to connect on a deeper level and ability to love. My precious gems, I don't care if your sexual experience has gold medals and is in the *Guinness Book of World Records*, sex does not cause men to love. It does bring two people close together and causes men and women to be sexually connected despite the rationale of it.

Sex, at times, can throw us into cycles of toxicity, dysfunction, and low value that cloud clear judgment. So, he treats me beneath who I am and cheats on me practically in my face… but because the sex is good, I stay. *(See "The Power of the P" – Sex overrated and undervalued)*

Although sensuality is critical and is what I refer to as "The Ultimate Synergy," if a man is emotionally unavailable, none of the above matters. Because the emotional part of him is blocked or unavailable, it resides elsewhere … whether it's another woman with whom he's still in love … whether it's the act of betrayal he endured that forced him to be guarded like Fort Knox, saying "I'll never give myself again" (although he still dates) … whether it's the mother that abandoned him or the father that rejected him … or whether it's that he was never taught how to connect with his emotions in a healthy manner.

This is why sensuality is critically important because it's the skill we (women) use for proper assessment and to allow proper timing! Anything of substance that is built to last shouldn't be rushed but should be a continual, consistent flow.

My loves, the **palate cleanser** is the pivotal point in your experience. This course determines whether you've set yourself apart to move forward or if you will put out a missing person's report…because he went ghost *(lol)*. He will either draw close, pull away—or in some cases, run away. Guess what, my love? Either decision he makes is fine, as you must understand that another's actions is no indictment on your value and who you are as a woman.

Let's say... you get to this point (palate cleanser) and you've already slept with him during the appetizer course *(which in my opinion was way too soon)* ... He may still walk away, but now he's walking away with a piece of you! This, my love, is why we must be attentive and safeguard our space.

Some men just aren't ready for a committed relationship or desire what you desire... period. If they aren't, that's okay. What isn't okay is when we, as women, fail to assess actions and/or feel that we can make a man what we desire them to be, which my love is a poor conclusion that yields destruction, deception, delusion, and heartbreak. *#Nogreenbeans #Bewise*

In total transparency, my gems and jewels, this pivotal palate cleanser meal course has disappointed me at times. This is the course where some men have walked away because the experience of who I am appeals to a certain palate ("taste bud"), one that they didn't have and didn't care to have. Can I tell you, jewels, that a man can be very attracted to who you are physically yet not have a clue who you are dimensionally? They may want "green beans," but, my love, I don't have any "green beans" aside from my "Ultimate 5-Course Experience."

This course determines whether you've set yourself apart to move forward or if you will put out a missing person's report...because he went ghost (lol)

This has been conflicted at times, primarily due to my decision to live a pure and celibate existence, to which I've been committed for 7 years since I divorced. I am continually committed, resolved, and reserved for my priestly king (husband)—and I want to be "preserved" for him also. Beloved, we are sacred. A sacred "ultimate experience" should be conservative with her precious assets. We were not designed and created to have men be in, out, up, down, and all around! Was I a bit disappointed and even frustrated at times because I desired connection and even liked a few of them? Absolutely, I was, my love! Was I willing to abandon my process and compromise my value to have a man around? Absolutely <u>not</u>!

Beloved, we are sacred. A sacred "ultimate experience" should be conservative with her precious assets.

Again, this is the importance of discovering our value because sometimes we (ladies) compromise for various reasons: our age, where we are in life, or because we don't want to be lonely and want to be loved. I get it, sis… we were designed for love, but guess what? I would rather have a lasting, quality connection than do something to pass time. *#NGB #Theultimate5courseexperience #Hugs*

Course Three

The Salad

Chapter 8
May I Speak with Your Manager Please?
(This is not what I ordered)

Can I let you in on a secret? ... My daughters often tease me and tell me I'm too particular when dining. They say I sometimes "complain" too much and should just let some things go. Can I tell you, gems? ... I sometimes try; however, having the privilege, opportunity, and blessing to have been reared and developed by the epitome of hospitality in the person of my late, revered, and dearly missed grandmother "Goldie" doesn't always afford me the opportunity ☺.

Since the 1970's, my grandparents were the owners and operators of the endeared vegetarian family restaurant in Philadelphia known as "The Patterson's." I can remember at 4- and 5-years-old, my project of the day was not to play outside, but rather snap fresh green beans in preparation for the day at the restaurant.

I have very fond memories of my Graham, including when she would send someone to the store. Everyone knew that if she asked for mayonnaise, she meant Hellmann's—not the store brand, not Kraft, not any other kind except Hellmann's. She was very particular and peculiar about ingredients because she knew it affected the presentation of the dish she was preparing. If she needed honey, it had better be Golden Blossom premium pure honey…why? Because she knew the results she needed.

Several of my grandmother's qualities were gifted to me, one of them being elevated hospitality. I absolutely love, love, love a great dining experience from the greeting…to seating…to service…to the ambience…to the meal itself. For me, all the above contribute to the dining experience. With that said, I beg to differ with my daughters' opinions. I'm not a complainer; I simply anticipate and expect what I prepare, invest, and show up for☺.

Normally, if I go grab a pizza, the expectation is that of a pizza parlor; however, I feel hospitality and customer service should be on the level you represent. McDonald's is considered "fast food," and in essence, Chick-fil-A is also, except they refer to themselves as "quick service." Chick-fil-A's elevated hospitality, amongst other amenities, is what separates it from the rest. If I go into a 5-star steak house and my server greets me with a warm towel for my hands and pulls out my chair, it's the same customer service, just different expectations based on the level that is represented.

There have been times I've tried a new restaurant or new dish, and it wasn't what I expected because I didn't know <u>what</u> to expect. I simply alerted my server, and as a courtesy, they apologized, offered to remove the entrée, and asked If I'd like to have another choice. There have also been times when I've been to spots that I frequent and enjoy. I place my order for my preferred choice, and when it arrives, it's not the quality that it generally is to have made my preferred choice list. The server may remove the dish, but then a few things follow: the manager visits the table, offers an apology, and personally asks if there is another entrée I would like or would I like a duplicate of the first. Upon my response, the manager also brings out the new entrée and, in some cases, removes the entrée from the check. There are other times when you must return an item and request to see a manger for reasons, including but not limited to cold food, wrong item served, hair or other object found in food, poor quality, entrée took an extensive time to be served, poor service, etc.

What warrants an item to be returned? Simply, because, it's not what you ordered. The only way an entrée can be returned for being the wrong item is if you "know" what you desire…you know what you ordered…you know what your order should look and taste like… Why? Because you've had it before.

My gems, it's the same in dating and relationships. How many times do we keep something that isn't what we ordered? Let me ask a more specific question, "How can you know what to return and what to keep if you have no clue what you desire…what it looks like…how it tastes, etc.?" Remember, my jewels, discovering our value is our pre-requisite.

When I am aware of my value, I know and can communicate my desires…what I like…what I dislike…what will compliment me and what wont. If you have no idea what you ordered (your desires), then it gives others permission to come aboard and give you what they desire, which in some instances can make you sick. *(See Call the Paramedics chapter.)*

My loves, we have discussed assessment all throughout this journey because it is necessary! Assessment is how you are able to decide to keep him or send him back. When meeting someone pay attention for red flags. I didn't say be weird and begin looking for them *(lol)*; I said be mindful and pay attention. If you notice a thing (or two) that causes you to raise an eyebrow, continue to watch and assess <u>in silence</u>. This doesn't mean to ask him a million questions; it means watching his nonverbal behaviors, translating his <u>actions</u>. You can answer your own questions by watching carefully, <u>not</u> fearfully or being weird *(lol)*.

For the record, my gems, a man can tell you anything, and sometimes he will, just to keep you around. Learn to pay attention and assess his actions! #*Nogreenbeans*

I'll give an example... I love and prefer a strong, resilient, authoritative, alpha man, who also has the discipline to be <u>gentle</u> with me. I don't care for violent, controlling, arrogant, cocky men, just not my cup of "tea." If I meet a man and we begin hanging out (gathering data), I'm watchful...how he handles others...how he handles disappointments...how he handles me.

Ladies, I used to disclose the type of man I felt I was most compatible with; I don't anymore. I found out that some men would try and morph into whatever I wanted, in efforts to get me. Most times, that was a detriment and led to disappointment. What you'll discover on the journey is that some men don't know what they want, and as a result, they are willing to do whatever. When, sometimes, they can't keep it up, it's because it was "something" they attempted to do but wasn't who they were. There is a difference!

I would rather he <u>be</u> a kindhearted person rather than <u>do</u> random acts of kindness because the man is trying to win you. Some gems may ask, "What's wrong with him trying to do something to please you?" There isn't anything wrong with it, *per se*; however, when people are different at their core than what they portray, it could be inauthentic, and after a while it will show.

If I notice signs of a controlling man that desires to dominate and subtly demand my time—continually putting emphasis on how he can provide for me financially, not interested in my goals and dreams, and basically wanting to do everything "for" me and not build "together"— (for me, loves) these are "return to senders."

I can hear some of you saying, "If a man wants to take care of me, I will allow him, with no problem!" Yes, my love, it sounds good; however, assessment is vital because remember, women of value are committed to their personal development which is inclusive of financial development and stability. Keep in mind I am speaking of someone new, not a longstanding relationship. The determining factor if something should be returned or not is governed by your value and your desires.

For me, although I have in the past, I would never, ever under any circumstances have any intimate involvement with a married man. Why? Because another woman's husband is not what I ordered (desire) ... sharing a man in any capacity is not what I ordered (desire) ... being alone for the holidays when I just slept with him two days prior is not what I ordered (desire) ... being a secret is not what I ordered (desire) ... being strung along is not what I ordered (desire) ... him not being available when I need, want, or desire him is not what I ordered (desire) ... living with the detriment and delusion of compromise, translated to mean he'll never leave his wife and even if he does and marries me, I will now become her (the mistress) that's built on lies, deceit and mistrust is not what I ordered (desire).

I, personally, have cut off all communication with men when I learned they were separated and living in two separate homes. *Why?* For me, jewels, the man is still married, and the law says so. I am one who has honor, respect, and reverence for covenants (marriages). I feel what missing is your assessment of the situation.

I know, I know, I know...there are some marriages that are basically dissolved; they are roommates, and that's the extent.... I also know how vulnerable both men and women can find themselves in marriages when there's nothing between them except time, expenses, and children.... I also know how easy it is to develop an emotional affair through someone simply listening to your heart.... I also know how vulnerable one can become when his/her spouse doesn't get him/her, doesn't pay attention to him/her, mistreats him/her, etc. I also know what it's like to have simply outgrown someone because when the time came to develop and grow together, one person didn't; therefore, the two grew apart.... I know (in the way of the world to some) it's nothing but a piece of paper, and that's why some have found themselves as live-in girlfriends for 5-6-7 years or more....

Please, my loves, don't misinterpret my opinion and <u>my</u> heart's desire for passing judgment, as I'm not. But I would admonish that if you've settled or compromised for something that isn't what you ordered (desired), you should send it back. There are some women that are resolved in the above—that marriage is just a piece of paper— and it's a mutual choice for the relationship to progress as such without marriage. That's totally okay, and I respect that decision. However, there are women who are in long term relationships who desire to be married and have been waiting and waiting for the man to become "ready," and it's been 5-7 years.

My loves, if you must force or coerce a man into being with you in any capacity, then, my precious gem, you've already lost with him. Meaning, he's already conquered too soon with no boundaries or accountability.

My love ask any man you trust what the deal is with this. He will tell you that the man is simply not ready, doesn't have a desire to, and will more than likely never be ready. Normally, what happens at this point is the women either relinquishes her value in silence and deals with it or gives an ultimatum.

Beauties, I personally don't give ultimatums, nor do I feel they are beneficial in relationships. My loves, if you must force or coerce a man into being with you in any capacity, then, my precious gem, you've already lost with him. Meaning, he's already conquered too soon with no boundaries or accountability. If this is where you are, precious, please don't be upset with me, as the first step to transformation is accepting our truth. Remember, this isn't a book; it's a transformational tool.

If he decides to give in to the ultimatum, my beloved gem, you must question, "Is this something he truly wants or is he merely responding?" Another question is, "Who is really liable? ... Could it be him because he's been stringing you along or could it be you because his words were allowed to be louder than his actions or had complete complacency pitched a tent with you both?" My loves, may I give a suggestion please? When a situation calls for an ultimatum, it's best for you to make the decision and exit the car.

Do you know the power of sisterhood? Of course, you do! Think about the irreversible, inseparable bond between you and your biological siblings and/or your sister-friend(s). Can I be totally transparent, my gems and jewels? It hurts me to see how we, as women, disrespect one another…are jealous of one another…sleep with one another's husbands/men…are shady towards one another…and will go to bat with one another, all over a man who, in some cases, is playing the game with everyone.

Did you know that, in most cases, men won't fight each other over a woman? What they <u>will</u> do is see who can go the farthest, or simply say he is finished.

Women? We will set the other woman up, have our friends stalk her, proceed to demean and disrespect her, will glorify and brag that her man is with another woman, and well you know the Title of the song, "You like 9-5; I'm the weekend.

My precious gems and jewels, can I suggest that maybe, just maybe, we are a part of the of the issue with our kings and priests? I wonder what would happen if we respected women, whether we know them personally or not. If a man approaches you that is married or in a relationship, I wonder what would happen if you sent him home. I wonder what would happen if we respected our fellow woman in her absence, as if she were our sister. I'm inclined to believe that a part of the reason our kings and priests are in the condition they are is because we allow it.

What about the emerging narcissistic personality? Ladies, have we even researched what the traits are, to compare if some or all are present in a person? This, my loves, should be accompanied with assessment. Narcissism is a personality disorder (more commonly in men) in which a person has an inflated sense of self-importance. Symptoms include an excessive need for admiration, disregard for others' feelings, an inability to handle any criticism, and a sense of entitlement.

According to *Psychology Today*, the Narcissist generally tends to have a sexual advantage in bed and uses the skill as a form of manipulation to hook his/her victims intentionally. It's only when they are certain that they have gained control of the person that their true colors begin to appear. The Narcissist is also known to be controlling and psychologically abusive, however, will diffuse the insults and abuse with intermittent affection, which is what the victim is trained to desire.

Is the Narcissist capable of love? A fact is that the Narcissist can cut off painful feelings and self-soothe to protect themselves from the hurt, pushing away feelings of love that they may feel for someone. They are utterly handsome, charming, and chivalrous, and their intent is to gain control to fulfill their own voids.

Gems, being patient and watching is critical! I repeat, critical! It's when we rush into things, full speed ahead, being led by our emotions…you know the emotions that since we were little girls and had visions of fairy tale love? … We cannot love without thinking.

We are living in a marketing and branding age, so much so that entrepreneurs, companies, and organizations spend upwards of 10's, even 100's, of thousands of dollars to learn the power and the art of persuasive influence to increase their brand awareness and sales. The psychology of words and colors in the branding/marketing industry are designed with one primary goal: to entice.

My gems, this can also be the same with men. They may invest a lot in themselves for one purpose: to persuade and influence. Not every man desires "to win the game," which is to be with you; some simply want to "score," which is to use you at their will, and some are oblivious to the difference. Some think scoring is winning the game when a man's goal is to sleep with you. Once he's conquered, he's won the game because sex was his goal and not a committed relationship of any kind. My jewels, please beware of the manipulator—the one who will say, do, and present whatever it takes, not to win the game (which is "you") but to simply "score" (which is what pleases him).

No Green Beans

Chapter 9

What's your Rating?

"What are people saying?"

Whenever I'm looking to explore something new—be it a restaurant, product, hotel, merchandise, or service—my first stop is the reviews. Why do I and so many others do this? Primarily, because when there is no frame of reference, your decision can be influenced (negatively or positively) by what **others** are saying. How did I hear about the place? Was it word of mouth? Is it a place I've always wanted visit? Is it the new trending spot because of their unsurpassed quality of cuisine, ambience, and service?

Reviews, ratings, and recommendations are paramount these days. It's the only place one can go to get real answers from real people and sometimes real photos to accompany! Reviews are critical for businesses or establishments—so much so that you are asked after a service is rendered, a training or customer service call, to leave a review of your experience. Reviews are where credibility rises and falls. The bottom line is people want to know what others are saying: Period!

What are the ratings and reviews of your establishment? "My establishment?" you might ask. Yes, my love, you should consider yourself an establishment. What is an establishment? It's a place where an organization operates, and you, precious jewel, are that organization (a 5-course experience). You're an empire, and here's is your organizational chart:

Oftentimes, either consciously or subconsciously, we place more value on the ones at the top (the CEOs, the ones out front), and I understand; however, there is something to be gleaned from the one that "appears" to be at the bottom. You've heard that any organization or CEO is only as good as the team around them. As you glance at the chart, you'll notice at the bottom are our experiences, failures and vulnerabilities, and learning curves, which are in essence the gold-star employees who make it all happen and give us the foundation and weight needed to build upon. They are the driving force behind our growth and are at the helm, ready to fulfill the mission. Just think…when you place an order with Amazon and expect your delivery, you look for the delivery driver who has your merchandise, which certainly is **not** Jeff Bezos, Amazon's CEO.

What's your Rating? 103

When you have a clear understanding of the quality of the product that you possess, you understand you must also use proper risk management to protect you from a major loss.

Do you not know, queen that it's the things at the bottom— the things we'd rather forget about, the things we wouldn't dare tell anyone because we're too ashamed—it's those things that when dealt with and healed from, give us the strong, firm foundation on which we build ourselves, brick by brick. Well, my jewels, because we understand the value and the vastness (massive, huge, limitless) of our organization, we understand that as we build on solid foundations, our experiences, triumphs, learning curves, failures, and vulnerabilities drive our growth.

This is when I hold myself accountable in that place to where I've worked intensely to arrive. My commitment and investment in myself yielded a ROI (return on investment) of 110%, which resulted in my discovery of the valuable asset that I really am. When you have a clear understanding of the quality of the product that you possess, you understand you must also use proper risk management to protect you from a major loss. *(That's another topic for another time.)*

In the Foreign Exchange market (FOREX), some traders use a risk management tool called a "stop-loss." A stop-loss is put in place, not to prevent one from entering a trade but rather, to protect the trader from a total loss should the market go in the opposite direction from what was projected. When a stop-loss is applied to a trade, you may lose currency but not to the extent that you would have had you not used proper risk management.

What am I saying? Gems, when dating we must use risk management. This doesn't mean that we don't attempt it but that we have perimeters (boundaries) in place to protect ourselves should things go in an unpredicted way. Remember, women of value are women of courage! They aren't afraid to be vulnerable; women of value don't wear masks because they simply have nothing to hide. In addition, they possess a level of self-awareness; if any faults, mistakes, etc. are made, they heal and are used as foundational strength.

Another critical component to your organization is your mission statement, which is a short summary of what your organization does and why it exists. It identifies the goal of your operations; it identifies the type of product or service you provide; it identifies your primary customers or market(s); and lastly, it is your distinction among others.

Gems, it is critical to understand "why" we exist; because if we lack the awareness of "why" we exist, it strips us from the awareness of "what" we are to do with our existence. At this point, we wander aimlessly and carelessly, which creates a void of direction. When we have a void of direction, it invites and allows others to come in and take us where they please—in some cases: a dead end, a vicious cycle, reckless driving, doing 90-mph in a 65-mph zone, and possibly breaking down on the side of the road. These are a few reasons why our "pre-dining experience" (introduced at the beginning of this reading) is a foundational pre-requisite.

Your mission statement should be equivalent to your purpose in life, why you exist, and how you operate in that existence. Remember, jewels, we are committed to becoming women of value who endeavor to live our lives from the inside (internally) out; we're analyzing the purpose and intent of our heart, our thoughts, our behaviors, our motives, our capacity to give rather than receive *(not to be confused with not receiving at all)*. Are my motives and actions self-seeking and self-serving only? Do I give <u>only</u> when there's a return for me?

Your mission statement should be inclusive of the products and services you provide. A woman of value has a purpose that's greater than who she is; her mantra is to take the high road, whether she feels like it or not. She won't be caught slashing tires, degrading other women or men; she doesn't plot, plan, and scheme; she doesn't hurt people intentionally; she doesn't "get back" at others, being devious and spiteful; she doesn't waste time and energy on counterproductive things that drain and devalue her. She will walk away first (intact) because women of value create their environments and are protective against intruders. She understands what it took to build her organization (self) and, therefore, refuses to allow anything or anyone to take her to a place that doesn't add or multiply to who she is: *It's their loss.* Women of value don't merely go with the flow; they <u>are</u> the flow!

Her products and services include resilience. She's a philanthropist (donor, sponsor, promoter), not limited to finances; she's committed to adding to others' lives. Therefore, she gives as if she's never been taken advantage of; her intent is to love as if she's never been hurt…to find and magnify the best in others…to enlarge and add value to whatever or whomever is in her sphere of influence, whether it be her children, partner, family, colleagues, strangers, friends, etc. <u>She's</u> liberated; therefore, she esteems others. She exudes love, confidence, kindness, respect, honor, understanding, forgiveness, <u>and</u> is wise enough to have boundaries in distribution.

I know, gems, I know… I hear you: "I'm tired of giving to people, and they don't' give the same in return", "I'm tired of my kindness being taken for weakness", "I need to see what you are bringing to the table first", "I'm not a fool", "I'm not doing that", "People don't appreciate you when you're nice", "I treat people how they treat me" and the list goes on. I know, I know, precious jewels, but can I share something with you please? Our commitment to be the best version of "<u>self</u>" isn't predicated upon what people do to us or how they treat us.

Because a woman of value has awareness of who she is, her goal is not to be all things to all people. She clearly understands that not everyone has access to her and not everyone can or will appreciate the true gem that she is; therefore, she doesn't allow anything to compromise who she is as a person. Rather, she removes herself from those who can't or refuse to see who she is. She's a rarity; she's a wow factor, not merely because of the heads she turns when she physically enters a room *(nothing wrong with that...wink)* but also because of the priceless treasure that comes through in her speech, communication, actions, and being! A woman of value understands—in the delectable words of our Forever First Lady Michelle Obama—"When they go low, we go high."

Inclusive with your mission statement are your goals, which should be <u>clearly</u> defined: What do you desire out of your "higher-self," not your "lower-self"? Ladies, we all have a lower version and higher version of self.

Our lower version is the version that doesn't make any investment or initiative for personal growth. Our "lower-self" does things because we "feel" like it, however, yields low results. Our lower version does the same things expecting different results. Our "lower-self" allows people to mishandle us and then make delusional excuses for their behavior. Our "lower-self" lacks the confidence to go after what we desire in our lives in any capacity.

Our higher version of self is disciplined, not perfect. Our "higher-self" is willing to look at the lower version of ourselves and command *her* to come up!! Our "higher-self" holds our "lower-self" accountable without justifications. Our "higher-self" does not allow any part of us to play small. Our higher version is working on our value, understands our value, and ultimately presents value!

Your mission statement should include your core values, which are the substance on which you are built. If the foundation of our organizational chart above (our trials, processes, etc.) has done its due diligence, then it should yield some introductory *values* equivalent to dependability, reliability, loyalty, commitment, open-mindedness, consistency, honesty, efficiency, etc. Our core values should drive our relationships so that we offer the best (our highest self), expecting the best and attracting the best.

"Situationships" … "It's complicated" … "It's whatever" … "Friends with benefits" *(oh and by the way, jewel, it's not a "benefit" to have casual sex for months or years with no accountability)* ... Precious jewel, it's impossible to show up as the irresistible, incomparable woman of value that you are with this level of behavior. It's not because the value isn't there but because you've simply yet to discover it.

How do we know when we've yet to discover our value? We begin by assessing our relationships, situationships, and the ones that are "complicated" in terms of how we initiate or respond. Are you initiating the majority of contact? If you are, sweetheart, I'd like for you to do a serious introspection right now, and I can guarantee, somewhere along the way, he's lost respect or never had it to begin with. Please don't confuse a man sleeping with you with him respecting you. Remember, gems, it's our responsibility to present ourselves in a way that brings value, or the lack thereof.

To add insult to injury, a man can tell (sooner than we think) what "type" of lady/woman we are. How do you conduct yourself when just meeting someone or becoming newly involved? Are you dehydrated, therefore acting "thirsty"? Is your conversation/action/body language rooted in sexual connotation? Is your attire, when you see him (physically or via facetime), overly sexual and way too exposed so that it brings attention to your body too fast and to soon? Let's not forget, kings are visual—they can't help it.

My loves, while some may think this is sexy and use it as bait, it's actually laying the foundation for him to see you primarily for sexual encounters. Am I saying that you shouldn't flirt, be feminine in your attire, and ultimately want him to desire you? Absolutely not. What I am saying is that when we present ourselves in one dimension (a side of "green beans") and not offer the other dimensions (more important delicacies on our menu), we do an injustice to ourselves, which prevents the man from seeing and being attracted to us in <u>totality</u>. Totality is what enables and triggers the man to connect on a deeper level.

I don't know about you queens, but I would rather have a man attracted to my brilliance, my smile, my heart, my thought process and the other countless attributes I possess, than to how good I am in bed. You're worth sooo much more! Why am I minimizing sex? I'm glad you asked *(wink)*. I'm not minimizing, jewel; I'm merely prioritizing. *#NoGreenBeans #NGB*

> *Is your attire, when you see him (physically or via facetime), overly sexual and way too exposed so that it brings attention to your body too fast and to soon?*

What do your reviews (meaning those that have encountered you) say about who you are? I'm not speaking of the shallow, mediocre question of "How good are you in bed?" review. What would they say of your attributes? ... your femininity and poise? ... your capacity to connect where it counts? How easy or how much of a chase you are? Are you even remembered or are you unforgettable? What do your reviews say about your ability to stimulate on an intellectual plateau? What do your reviews say about your kindness and the capacity of your heart? What do your reviews say about your ability to "make a man behave" and desire you even more because you set a standard? If they've conquered too soon, my love, the chase is over, and they're off in search of the one who can capture them.

What impression do you leave on those that have experienced you, and most importantly, what are they saying to others? Ladies, you know men talk the same way we do ☺. If your name comes up in a male's conversation, what's being said? Now, I hear some my beautiful ladies saying, "It doesn't matter what others say about me," and guess what, jewel? To a degree that may be correct; however, we're not talking about Siskel and Ebert critics; we are talking about those that have experienced for themselves.

Precious gems, if we are resolved and committed to being 100% authentic, who is one that lives from the inside out, then we have to muster (gather) the maturity, courage, and confidence required to accept that what people say about us "does" matter, but…here's the caveat…only if there is validity to what's been said.

My beautiful gems, please remember to be patient with yourself and your process. As stated in the introduction of this writing, there are plenty of things I have done that didn't bring honor to myself or my precious, priceless body. Understand that we're not perfect, and because we're all growing, learning, and transforming into the "Five-course experience," it's a place we must <u>emerge</u> (develop) into. (*Hugs!*) *#NoGreenBeans* #Theultimate5courseexperience #NGB

Chapter 10
The Boss Chick Movement

"My Concern"

According to CNBC, there are 12.3 million women-owned businesses that have collectively generated over $1.8 trillion per year, translation: we are among the top earners. We are no longer confined to cooking, cleaning, ironing ties, and rearing children as full-time "salaried" positions.

Please don't misunderstand my statement. I totally believe in a woman serving her family (as they shouldn't be neglected) and having ultimate delight while doing so. If the family dynamic is structured where the woman cares for the home while the man cares for all things financial, by all means, work it! There's no right or wrong, good or bad; it's simply different and preference.

However, I would like to add a caveat…if you're a woman and you desire to pursue your dreams and goals but feel like you can't due to your children and husband, then, my love, may I recommend you intentionally and strategically discover or rediscover the fragments of your life and piece them back together, as you've gotten lost in the mix. Your children won't be young forever. Once you've sacrificed for everyone else, you start to ask, "Who's sacrificing for me?" You owe it to yourself, my love! Go pursue your dreams! Yes, of course, every parent wants the best for their children, and of course, sometimes there's delayed gratification; however, let it be delayed rather than non-existent and merely something "You've always wanted to do."

Since we're here, may I kindly suggest something to any married or relational woman who has lost or has yet to discover her voice in the relationship? What do I mean? You rarely say anything; you rarely speak about how you feel and your desires, and when you do, it's minimized and/or overlooked. You also, my love, could benefit from becoming the "Ultimate 5-Course Experience." A relationship is not one-sided, and some of us gems and jewels have lost our voice in relationships. Find and amplify your voice! You matter, precious gem *(Hugs)*.

I know I came out of the gate full speed ahead, however, felt it necessary. Let's continue☺.

Who runs the world? Girls! You know the saying: "Behind every good man is an incredible woman." Even husbands will tell you that their wives really run things but make them feel like they do ☺. We've confirmed and solidified this several times throughout this writing. Women are preferred by design and desire, not default.

Women have the "It-Factor": our thought process…our execution…our ability to multi-task…our abilities to love, to build, to affirm…our ability to receive a sperm cell and birth a human being…our ability to communicate our feelings and help men discover theirs *(lol)*…our ability to make a man feel like the luckiest man on earth merely with our presence…our ability to rear children…build businesses…help men build theirs…profit millions of dollars for other companies…provide therapy when needed…act as a coach when someone is off task…and we can go on and on.

Women don't have to "oversell" themselves. The proof is in the pudding! We've established that. The way we are manufactured and wired and the way we move can have our kings and priests adoring us, looking at us and saying "How do you do it all?"—desiring us even the more, needing us, and yes, my loves, sometimes even being intimidated by us.

As the world turns, we are experiencing more and more women rising in the seven spheres of society: religion, family, education, government, media, arts, and business. The woman is powerful and influential! That cannot be denied. However, my loves, I feel we could benefit from learning to properly leverage our influence and power as it relates to men.

Yes, I know, I know, I can hear you ... some of my gems may say, "I'm not dimming my light for anyone.... God made me to shine; I'm not shrinking for anyone.... I need a strong man; if you he can't handle me, then I'll find someone who can—Good-bye..." and a plethora of other thoughts.

My precious jewels, I totally understand and agree to a certain extent. I am by no means suggesting that you shrink to make others feel comfortable; what I am saying is that, oftentimes, our nonverbal language shows as well as our verbal language. Men were created and designed to feel "needed"; it's their makeup. *Why?* Because they are our protectors, providers, and leaders. They are built for productivity, and when we come along and play superwomen and get the "I-got-it" syndrome, it rips the "superman cape" that they so desperately desire to use with us.

Whether you are an entrepreneur or an executive in corporate, you call the shots; you make things happen; the majority come to you for decisions and not the other way around. You make the final review before approval, and you see the payoff in your profits! Girl, you're getting it! That's excellent! I'm proud of you! However, some of us have not learned or even desire to learn how to "leverage" our power between our career and our beloved.

So, what happens? You subconsciously (or consciously) speak to your beloved as if he's an employee or someone on the team. Your actions speak, "I really don't have time, and you'll have to get on my calendar," which translates to he's not a priority for you. He rarely, or never, gets invited into your world, so he feels like a "third-wheel" to your business. What do I mean? Jewels, do you realize the impact of intentionally letting a man know "you need him" and not only to pay bills and spoil you? Do you know what honor, respect, and affirmation does for a man? It does the same thing that safety, security, exclusive love, and provision does for us!

Even if you already know the answer to something, ask him anyway! Make him feel needed, included, desired, and valued; Oh, and when he offers his opinion and/or suggestion, take it and use it! *(Lol)*

My loves, when we are in our element of sparkle, we sometimes may not realize that our beloved feels like an outsider, neglected or just there. Think about it, ladies… if we are earning 6- and 7-figures, calling the shots in our spheres of influence, and holding it down, I can see a man wondering where he fits in.

In recent years, I've heard more and more women say, "I don't need a man." Yes again, my loves, I'm with you. I get it. I don't need a headache, chaos, and/or to be mishandled and undervalued either, but when I think about it, connection and partnership are beautiful, powerful tools in the earth—when two mature people are inclusive in it! Two are better than one! We were designed to co-dominate! Yes, Yes, and Yes… it must be right and mutual ☺.

I must say that my concern is that we have reduced the value of the man to financial means only, and there's much more value to a man than what he brings financially or the lack thereof, although it is important.

Gems, I will yet agree when we concur that the "state" of the man is scarce. However, going back to our foundational tools—one being for us to take responsibility for our actions—we have a responsibility to value the man in his totality.

In my previous marriage, I learned to live out what has become one of my favorite passages in my favorite book: The Bible ☺. In Proverbs 14:1, it states, "A wise woman builds her house, but a foolish one tears it down with her _own_ hands." How many times have we torn our homes (men) down? My love, I admonish you to be wise and "build" your house. Guess what? If your home consists of a man that's present…well, my love, you have a responsibility to build him also! Remember, that's what boss chicks do… we don't only build businesses, capital, profits, and bank accounts; we build our kings and priests, our children, other women, and anyone else in our spheres of influence!

Another strategy that is useful in leveraging our influence and power is _vulnerability_. Vulnerability enables us to disclose fragile areas of ourselves that otherwise may be hidden and/or buried. Vulnerability creates trust, which in turn, activates the protector in a man. Sometimes, my loves, we can be controlling and manipulative when it comes to men; these self-sabotaging behaviors will active the peasant in him, not the priest, provider, and protector.

When in dialogue with my sisters, friends, uncles, cousins, male acquaintances, and male platonic friends (some of whom I've previously dated and some not), we often discuss current challenges of dating and/or becoming acquainted with someone. Most women say, "All men want is sex," and most men say, "All women want is money; they are phony, fake, immature, selfish, and plastic" (not only cosmetically but authentically, meaning they aren't their true-selves).

It was rather intriguing to me to hear men say they would like women to open up and be more vulnerable and transparent and not seem like they are hiding things. Gems, this could be as a result of us being guarded and careful with our hearts and who we let in, but it could also be a result of unresolved issues that we've not had the courage or refuse to deal with. It then presents and portrays a shallow, face-value portion of us. Not only do real men notice, but it's a red flag. No one is perfect, and men don't fall in love with perfect women, contrary to what we've been told. Embracing our imperfections is one of the most courageous, liberating gifts that we can give for ourselves because it eliminates the pressure and torment of needing to "perform" instead of being your authentic, perfectly imperfect self. ☺

My precious jewels, as we continually commit to our personal development, this is a gentle reminder that this is _not_, and I repeat, _not_ about men and their actions or lack thereof. Some of us have taken liberty and license to "Play the same game" as men, which is self-destructive. Gems, remember women are incubators; that means we are designed to receive, nurture, and cause growth, and guess what? It's the same when associating negative behaviors, thoughts, emotions, and wounds. I honestly believe when we, as women, take the courage to live our lives from the inside out, then (and only then) can we be transformed.

When we embody the "I-treat-men-how-they-treat-me" syndrome and use it in the same context, we are then putting our entire being (spirit, soul, body) into "traumatic shock." *Why?* Because we were not designed to behave like that. We are poised in femininity and grazed in grace. When we "force" our souls to shut down our paths of love and replace them with stones, rocks, debris, and rubble, we then subconsciously bury ourselves beneath it all and are not able to love or receive love; that my love is toxic. We were designed to cultivate and receive love. It's how we grow and blossom and bloom.

Honest question, jewels, "**H**ave you ever been involved with someone for whom you cared from a ***deep, dimensional*** place?" I mean a deep and dimensional place that if you're not careful and engaged in the relationship with heart **and** head, you could potentially lose yourself in that someone? Gems, there is nothing shallow about us *when* we show up in the full capacity of who we are! Yes, my loves, I'm certain we've all had shallow moments *(both of my hands are raised)* when our shallow thoughts led to even more shallow behaviors that resulted in low-value, subpar, and for some of us, embarrassing results.

Have you ever given your all? Have you ever invested all of you (emotionally, sexually, physically, financially, psychologically) in someone? I mean, for years or at least it seemed like it! You have been through highs, lows, ups, downs, from side to side, and everything in between. Have you ever looked at a man and thought to yourself, "I will hold him DOWN," meaning "I will be whatever he needs me to be?" *(Both hands raised again.)* "I'll push him to the next level…. I'll be an instrument of healing for him…. He's never had a woman like me!" Have you ever asked yourself "Why?" Let me be the first to say, my precious gem, you were not stupid; you merely needed to go through your process, discover and leverage ***your*** value, and show up in the full capacity of the ultimate experience you were created to be.

After many times of failing forward and learning from my experiences, I would ask myself, "Am I too kind? … Why do I desire to give, give, give regardless of what I get in return?" Gems and jewels, it goes back to who we are _to_ the man.

Some of my queens may beg to differ with what I'm about to say, and it's okay as I respect your opinion also... *(drum roll, please)* ... WE were **created for** the Man. Queens, our kings and priests need us in so many ways: they need us to affirm them... they need us to respect and honor them... they need us to believe in them... they need us to give birth to their legacy... they need us to tell them, "Baby, you can do it"... they need our presence for comfort, reassurance, and peace... they need our voice for therapy, soothing and even arousal... and, of course, we know they need sexual relations.

We were designed to love holistically, deeply, widely, continually, unconditionally and perpetually (never ending or changing). If our ability to do such has been tainted, halted, obscured, or jaded... well, my precious jewel, it can more than likely be traced back to some level of trauma in our past or present that we have yet to deal with or even acknowledge. How can I say this with confidence? Our love heals; however, the lack thereof can cause an opposite effect—to break.

Because we were created for them, our kings not only adore us, how about they can't live without us and deep down at their core, they know it! However, if his ability to love, cultivate, protect, and provide has been tainted, blocked, or jaded, trust and believe, precious jewels, it can be traced back to some level of historic trauma and/or event past that has yet to be addressed.

Men look at us in amazement *(lol);* they really do! We are reproducers. Imagine this... we receive the seed of a man into us and that tiny little seed, once incubated, reproduces a baby that goes from never existing to a full span of life to reach 70+ years! That's Powerful when you really ponder!

We are in a time where a huge portion of focus is financial gain, and if you can provide financially—and, in some cases, sexually—then you can behave in any way you choose. Men can simply pay their way into women's beds, and women can basically "use men" at their disposal because, after all, I don't need your money—I have my own. This breeds another fungus; we now have women being primary caretakers for men, which goes against the function by design.

My beautiful jewels let's boss up for sure; let's continue to make our mark in the earth. However, my challenge for us is to remain intact with the femininity and poise that bring respect and honor to men. I'm a believer that true holistic success is not money but rather WINNING in all areas of life. If you are "playing small" by showing up as a side-chick or lacking value, then that's not what success looks like. Moreover, we refrain from being a public success and a private failure. *(Luv Ya)*

Bonus:

Do you remember my conclusion was that the woman was created for the man? Do you also remember I told you my favorite book was the Bible? Well, here's a bonus:

Question: "How was the woman created for the man?"

In Genesis 2:18, we read of the one thing that was not declared "good" in all of God's creations: "Then the LORD God said, 'It is not good that the man should be alone.'" The same verse includes God's solution: *"I will make (create) him a helper (ideal partner) fit for him."* Eve was the solution to Adam's deficiency. Furthermore,

God's statement that it was <u>not good for man to be alone</u> implies that Adam was lonely and incomplete by himself. He had been created for relationship, and it is impossible to have relationship alone. With the creation of Eve, Adam experienced the joy of love for another person.

Course Four

The Entrée

Bonus
Real Men ~ Real Answers

Okay Ladies, here we go ~ Real Men; Real Answers!

I've spent a great deal of time gathering this content about the truth from men. I've personally engaged each man with what you will read below.

I intentionally brought commentary from our Kings & Priests so that you wouldn't take my word for it. Below are two (2) sections, one survey I completed of approximately 300 men and asked, "What are the top 3 things you need from your lady?" I recorded the answers below via percentage chart:

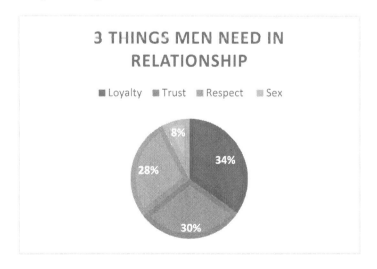

The survey was ***not*** multiple choice (intentionally) so the men could articulate their answers and not to be influenced by what was already noted (multiple choice). Which raises another question: "Are you able to *articulate* your desires?" If someone asked you what you like and dislike, would you be able to respond if there was no multiple choice? It's critical that we learn to communicate our desires; because if we don't then others will. #NGB

Ladies, loyalty and trust led the survey. Men need it! They must be able to trust a woman and feel safe with her, the same way we must feel safe. How about only 9% needed sex in their top 3? Did that surprise you? Well, it solidified a lot for me which is that despite what some say and think that all men want is sex, I must beg to differ. Yes, men desire sex, but it's not ***all*** they desire. There are some foundational "core" values that affect men differently which are trust, loyalty and respect and when you affect a man in a different way, it allows you my love to receive a different response. #NGB #Theultimate5courseexperience

Next, is my favorite! I asked a group of men, various ages, and status' what it takes for them to commit and/or be in a committed relationship. Their answers are below and were not altered at all. For confidentiality, their names are replaced with relationship status, age, and Industry. Hear ye, hear ye ladies: These are real answers from real men:

Divorced - Age 44 – Investor & Information Technology

Commitment isn't a word associated with the gender of a person but rather, how a person's feels about committing. Commitment can come in a variety of forms. The need for a man to commit varies on the type of man you are dealing with. If committal is on the low end of the totem pole and you sincerely want that man, it will be better served for you to get educated on why it is so low to help drive motivation. If his motivation isn't moved to commitment, don't set yourself up for failure and blame anyone else. On the opposite end of the spectrum, you will need nothing for a committed man to stay committed. Its internalized in him. Some are committed from religious stance and others are from upbringing. The in between men will need a combination of education, companionship, and motivation. Know the fruit of a man so you know what you're are getting into.

Married - Age 46 – Anesthesiologist

Once a man "fully commits" to a woman, he is not going anywhere. Men will seek for a woman until he finds the one that can draw that commitment out of him. The challenge comes in 2-fold: He hasn't found the one who's able to draw commitment out of him; even if he found that woman, the woman's desires may not be fulfilled in him, thus, they have different feelings. Every man can be "real" once they strongly feel they've found a woman to commit to a lifetime relationship with.

Loyalty, companionship, and knowing the woman has faith and is not going to get afraid when we pursue our goals especially when things doesn't go as planned is also critical with commitment.

Single – Age 44 – Music Producer

Most men with vision, purpose, and drive doesn't take long to commit to a woman when he knows purpose and vision are there. The challenge has been that most women only want a wedding and not the true covenant and purpose of marriage. It's difficult to find this in this present age we live.

Divorced – Age 46 – Pastor

There are three things a man needs in order to commit.

He needs a woman who he can continuously HUNT!! Some women give it all to soon and leave nothing for later. We want a woman who is outgoing and has a drive to continue to be better. A man will commit to a woman he can trust! A man will never commit to a woman he can't trust with his emotions, his heart and his ego. A man will commit to a woman who is willing to look at him as a King. Nothing makes a man feel better then when his woman looks to him to settle a matter or look to him for advice or security... remember we're God like.

My challenge with commitment has been **Quality** and all the above answers to question #1 to be honest I would love to be committed! But it must be right!!

Single – Age 42 – Author, Speaker

First, I believe a man must be in a spiritual and emotional space to be clear headed to first even want to commit.

Second, a man must first realize that it's even beneficial for him to decide to be with one woman. Third, I also believe coming into contact with the right woman will change a man's mind because she will have an effect that will have him in his thoughts and paying attention to how she's impacting his life, how she makes him feel, how he feels when he's in her presence, she's consistently on his mind and how his life has changed for the better since she's come apart of his life. Although; there are more women than men. There's a small quantity of women that are truly in connection with the gem that they are, but the sad part is those women run with men that's far from their atmosphere. One of my biggest challenges with commitment has been me to be honest. And It seems as if when I meet a woman and

I have an interest (which is far and few between), it seems to never work.

Divorced – Age 54 – Movie Producer

I've lived through some very challenging relationships and blessed to say I have learned much about commitment.

After 19 years of being married, 8 years in a very serious relationship, and being engaged twice, I can say with confidence that the most important thing for me to make a commitment to a woman would be that I'm LOVE WITH HER and SHE'S IN LOVE WITH ME. Yes!! I've been in relationships where one person may be in love and the other person is not! They will sometimes say, "YOU KNOW HOW MUCH I LOVE YOU!" That's not being IN love with me!! If you want me to commit, the connection must be mutual.

Divorced – Age 52 – Saxophonist

A man must be exhausted from the single life. That means he's tired of the chase, tired of dating different women, tired of games, tired of being alone though he's dating, tired of lying to himself and to the people he's dealing with. Tired of empty intimacy, exhausted from meaningless hangouts, ready to prefer someone's heart over his own desires. He must see her as someone that will make him a better person and that he will do the same for her. He must see her as someone he wants to be around every day. He must see her inward beauty as priceless. But most importantly he must know what love is. Like many men, I grew up with a single parent and didn't know what love was until I built a true relationship with Christ. Not that I did everything perfect afterwards, but it definitely took away my excuse for not knowing how to love and made me more accountable and responsible.

I am 2 years divorced and I am at an age where I am very mindful of the time I invest in a relationship and the quality of life that relationship will render. My challenge is not with commitment, I prefer a committed relationship. There are definitely things I need to work on that will make me more ready. For me I am looking for the commitment that happens organically. It's not pressured, it's not forced, it doesn't come with a lot of drama, I am not wondering and guessing about how you feel and what am I feeling but it happens so subtle that you never had to ask are we together or question if I love you because your heart and actions always said it for you. After intimacy you want that person to stay around, I know that may seem to be an awkward statement but it's true and most men would agree, if that's not the case she's not the one. More importantly the key for me is to find someone I can grow spiritually with. That is the bonding glue to a committed relationship.

Divorced – Age 54 – Pastor

Trust is a major part of my commitment requirement. She would have to be able to handle my humanity. Can I be safe to be myself, without any judgement. Her security in who she is but loves to impress me and give me that wow factor and I give her that wow factor! Her being genuinely into me and me genuinely into her!

Divorced – Age 53 – Pharmaceuticals

For me to commit would require a shared loyalty both intellectually and spiritually. The man needs to know can he deposit his loyalties and his vulnerabilities to a woman who can cover him and encapsulate these feelings in virgin love.

Divorced – Age 44 – Author & Entrepreneur

Commitment takes a willingness to be led by God through me and she has to smell like fire, meaning, I want to be assured just as myself, that she has been processed enough that she will humbly do introspection on herself when becoming unappreciative of even the smallest part heaven on earth I giving to her. I would need unwavering support and to be spiritually equally yoked.

Divorced – Age 44 – Pastor & Investor

For me to commit would equate to a woman having the skill to love me from a broken place, to understand where I've been and determine if she is ready and able to deal with a man in a place of recovery. Some men have challenges with commitment because a man needs to know if a woman desires them or what he can provide? Do you desire me or my status? Many women have said I was their husband and my question is: "If you're my rib-then what's your function?" If you say you are my wife then you should be in tune with what your function is in my life.

Gems & Jewels, this was just a few responses from men. As you can see, they differ regarding desire, but notice what men need is aligned across the board. Men aren't difficult and in no one's response did we hear "good sex" for commitment. Again, not minimizing sex, but certainly not maximizing it either. The men gave foundational responses that is necessary for them to love and commit ladies, because a man won't commit to a women with whom he doesn't have an emotional connection with. Hence is why we've seen responses like loyalty, consistency and being able to trust a woman with their vulnerabilities. These are areas that unlock the man cave (emotions).

Ladies, if we "assess", we can have a committed, lasting love. It's possible, real men still exist, and real love still exist. The caveat is doing assessment to determine and differentiate. To determine if you are aligned and on the same page as it relates to relationship. To differentiate, meaning to separate and know the difference between a man who is authentic and genuinely interested in you or a counterfeit who will morph into whatever he needs to be to score and end the game! #NGB #Nogreenbeans #Nocounterfeitsallowed

Chapter 11
Braised Artichoke Hearts

My Loves, at this juncture in our journey if we've assessed and made application, we should see a difference in dating and the caliber of men we entertain and attract, remember, we **discover** our value, **position** our value and **present** our value to **real men** who **desire pursue** and **capture.**

I know, I know, many believed that our main entrée was a sexual encounter when actually my gems, it's the dessert which is our final course – The **Icing** on the cake 😊.

The main course my darlings is a man's heart, **not** his genitals. A man's heart is what should be desired to capture for a lasting, committed love. When you have a man's heart, you have him holistically. It doesn't matter who comes and who goes, you have his heart. When you have his heart, you have his time, his energy, his commitment. Now, how is a man's

I have a question for you gems & jewels... If you had access to a man's heart would you know what to do with it?

heart captured you may ask. Well ladies, they've expressed it in the previous chapter.

I have a question for you gems & jewels… If you had access to a man's heart would you know what to do with it? Would you know how to care for it, including the fragile, broken, vulnerable, and yes, wounded areas?

Dealing with men at a dimensional level is an art my loves. Sometimes we deal with men and not "engage" men. We lack the capacity, depth and dimension to tap into necessary areas within them and that can be for several reasons of our own which we've previously discussed in our foundational pre-requisites chapter(s).

Did you know, we may have to act as skilled surgeons at times when dealing with the frailties of men or do you not have time for that or did you misinterpret that to mean he has issues or misunderstand his vulnerability to mean that he's weak when none of these are factual. Remember, a dimensional, lasting connection is not surface, and you must be tested to see if you can "care" for a man, I mean really care for him in a dimensional way. I'm speaking of the level of care that goes beyond preparing an exquisite meal, running bath water, lighting candles, meeting him at the door in attractive attire, giving massages and holding down things financially if necessary, although all of these are beneficial.

You can do all of the above for a man and still have no clue how to reach him dimensionally just as a man can do all the above for a woman and have no clue or desire to reach her dimensionally. Let's speak truth here, dimensions require depth, height and width. Dimensional connection is not shallow nor surface, moreover It requires both parties to have an "appetite" for something of depth. Ladies, even if his palate is used to something else and you introduce him to a new (your) dining experience, he may not only enjoy it, but may make it his preferred place to dine (wink).

Darlings, we must be a place of safety and comfort for a man to yield his heart, hence is why in the previous chapter, emphasis were placed on trust, loyalty, and respect. For a man to lay down his armor (his strength, his ego, his influence, his affluence), the place in which it's laid, must be a place that can handle **the weight** of his armor which is **"Who He Is"**, **not** what **he has** and **not** what **he does. There is a difference my loves in what a man does and who he is. #Assessment #Dimensions**

Oftentimes we as women lack the ability and skill to connect with a man via his emotions; we are trained to believe the "main course" and the way to man's heart is through sex (and meals). Contrary to the belief, capturing a man's heart is more beneficial for longevity.

Creating a "Safe Haven" for his heart, his armor and his TRUTH (acceptance) is guaranteed to capture his heart, however this is where we sometimes have challenges due to our own frailties and unresolved trauma in our history (see Toxicity chapter). Accepting a man for who he is, is liberating for you and him. Be his friend, not a conditional friend. Can he really tell you anything? It's can be somewhat challenging at times to be man's friend and lover at the same time, but sweetheart, that's where trust lives. Can you provide a no judgement zone where he can be himself?

Yes, men are strong, however if he gets weak sometimes, can he share it with you, or can you "assess" and coach him back to the place the strength and greatness? Yes, they're our protectors, however what happens if he's ever fearful and "yes", men get fearful and if he is, he shouldn't be emasculated. Yes, they're our providers, however what happens when he may not have it to provide, is he made to feel less than or even his efforts aren't good enough? My loves, we're talking about creating a safe place because if a man is processing and we lack the capacity to handle their frailties and vulnerabilities during that time, my love you've already lost him. You may not lose him sexually or even physically, but you certainly won't have him emotionally because ***his heart can't trust you***.

Jewels, another caveat is that women are emotional feelers and men are logical thinkers. They don't connect as easy as we do, but when they do... **they do!** However, if he's been hurt or betrayed, it's possible my loves, he may become emotionally ***unavailable*** to anyone else. It's the truth! They will still hang out with you, even see you, but the emotional pathway is closed off, and if they can't control the temperature of their feelings for you, then they may get ghost which is translated to ***"self-sabotage"***. Another skill is learning the ability to have patience with men, however, do assessment to ensure he's not playing games, but just needs a moment. Did you know that men have fears of giving their hearts to someone? Did you know that men sometimes have unresolved hurt, pain and betrayal that needs healing? Yes, I know we live in a "performance" driven world meaning things are solidified tangibly whether performance for people, social media, status, bucket lists, relationship goals, etc. Gems, I'm not minimizing that, however in true dimensional connection, there will be areas of you both that need attention. Oftentimes, men have unattended areas that may cause them to not to rush, be watchful or even pull away at times. This, my loves, isn't the same as toxicity and shouldn't be compared as such. When a man has areas that have gone unattended, it doesn't necessarily translate to he's no good; sometimes they have no clue because it's a sacred part of them that has either been compromised or yet to be discovered, hence is why assessment, patience and skill is needed and necessary for dimensional connection.

As a reminder darlings, ***we are discovering the best in us to present the best of us!*** #Nogreenbeans #NGB

Course Five

Dessert

Chapter 12
"The Power of the "P"

There was a song that Destiny's Child sang in the early 90's entitled, "Say my Name," which was actually one of my favorites during that time. The song spoke of the woman's desire for the man to say her name to basically prove his loyalty.

"What's up with this chapter title?" some may ask, and "What is 'The Power of the P'?" "The Power of the P" is an urban phrase that denotes the irresistible influence of a woman's super power, which is the sexual experience—the influence that creates both beautiful babies and deadly diseases (simultaneously), It's the irresistible influence that is the cause of pleasure and is rooted in pain, it's the irresistible influence that is both bought and sold, it's the irresistible influence of which men and women spend countless amounts of money, it's the irresistible influence for which couples are disloyal to their spouses, it's the irresistible influence that can break, bond, and bind, it's the irresistible influence that some women use to generate revenue, have all expenses paid, and control any man in their sphere of sexual influence. You know the song ladies, "Use what you got to get what you want."

This is the way sex is designed. It's the height of euphoria—the crescendo that causes one to be abused, manipulated, mishandled, verbally, mentally, and even physically abused. It causes one to love without thinking, to ignore rationality, to confuse clarity. Sexual intercourse, my loves, is designed to activate submission; that's why "chains" are so challenging to break: It breaks and ties souls.

Sex is a powerful connection, and, ladies, because of this (amongst other things) we have somewhat of an influence over men. *Why?* Because men **need** sex. I hear you ladies saying, "I need sex, too" *(lol)*, but I'm talking about the effect that sex has on the man.

Women, by design, were created to receive love, affirmation, cultivation, amongst other things. Men, by design, were created to receive love also, but theirs translates to respect, honor and, yes, sex.

Gems, when we honor and respect men, we are saying, "I love you" in their love language.

Gems, when we honor and respect men, we are saying, "I love you" in their love language. Yes, we all have love languages for how we give and receive love. For us to get the ultimate out of relationships, it's critical that we love the other person in their love language, not ours. For example, one of my love languages is receiving gifts. Just because I enjoy giving and receiving gifts doesn't mean that my beloved will feel valued and/or loved if I present him with a gift… W*hy?* Because that's not his love language. If his love language is "words of affirmation" and I continue to get him gifts, he will ultimately be unfulfilled in the relationship; I'm presenting him with what I "think" he desires because it's what "I" desire, and that's far from the truth. *(To learn more about love languages, I recommend Gary Smalley's brilliant, liberating book* The 5 Love Languages.*)*

Okay, back to sex… As we were discussing, it is a powerful interaction that I don't think we realize is sacred. Have you asked yourself why you are so "attached" to someone you know is toxic for you? You may have even admitted that you know they aren't any good, but the sex is. You may not have said it verbally; however, your actions are screaming it.

Jewels, as you know, one of our foundational tools is assessment. Once we can assess the "why" behind the "what," it yields greater clarity and understanding. Have you ever had a sexual encounter with someone you simply couldn't get over and walk away—regardless of how bad and toxic he was for you?

My loves, as previously stated, I intentionally and strategically live my life from the inside out so that means, I always, always, always want to know the "why" behind the "what." Assessing my thoughts and behaviors using this strategy was (and still is) extremely instrumental in my healing process and discovery of my value. It wasn't until I began to question myself, <u>out loud</u>, about the low level, toxic behavior in which I indulged. Questions like, "Why was I okay, comfortable, and complacent in the deception and delusion of dealing with another woman's husband?" … "Why was I okay with 'messing around' with someone, with no validity or identity in the relationship?" When you begin to hold <u>yourself</u> accountable, my love, that's when you begin to be transformed. When your higher-self, commands your lower-self to come higher, my precious gem, you are being transformed. This is necessary because sex can blind us, influence our decisions, and alter our emotions.

It is scientifically proven that sexual intercourse is as addictive as drugs, gambling, alcohol, etc. According to *Science Alert*, there are multiple hormones and neurochemicals that are released at the height of a sexual encounter (orgasm). There are two primary hormones. The first is dopamine: the hormone that is responsible for feelings of pleasure, desire, and motivation. Dopamine is the same hormone released related to food and several drugs. The second hormone that the brain releases during heightened intercourse is oxytocin: the hormone that makes us feel close to others and promotes affection. Oxytocin is also known as the bonding hormone because it's also released during breastfeeding and is known to facilitate a sense of love and attachment. Additionally (as a bonus), the prolactin hormone is released and is responsible for that feeling of satisfaction. It's also the main hormone responsible for milk production following pregnancy. These hormones can play different roles in our bodies and are part of the brain's way of strengthening our social connections.

Once I educated myself on the "why" behind the "what" of sexual engagement, it aided me in my process of healing and liberation, thus enabling me to make wise choices beforehand, which was "assessment" and not acting on impulse.

Beautiful gems, when the primary part of your influence in a man's life is through his sex organs, the dopamine in his brain and the release of oxytocin makes him feel like he's addicted…and guess what, ladies? He very well may be… but he's addicted to the way you make him feel sexually, not who you are as a person. So, that's why he can stay with his family and slide in an out of your apartment whenever he feels like it—after hours or "in between" hours. My love… #NGB (sigh)

Now that we've discussed the scientific effect of sex on the brain and understand why sex is so influential, I'd like to discuss our upcoming chapter "Real Men—Real Answers," which is devoted to our kings and priests. We will hear from real men with real answers about their opinions of love, commitment, sex, and what they desire out of relationships. I thought it noteworthy to include this chapter because I didn't want to merely give you my "opinion" from a woman's point of view—although I have over 20 years of experience *(yes, I began early* ☺*)*, but rather I wanted you to also hear directly from men.

As stated, I have several male platonic friends with whom I discuss men, women, relationships, and the like. You have no idea how many of my friends tell me that they literally have to push women away, translated to turning away sex. I have a friend who told me he was training a woman in the gym once, and at the end of their first session, she grabbed him, hugged him and said, "You know you can get this whenever you want." My precious gems and jewels, we have extensive internal work to do if our kings and priests must tell us "no" and redirect us.

My love, if you are reading this, I want you to know that you are worth so much more! Your body is a precious and valuable commodity; furthermore, you deserve to be loved, honored, cherished, and adored. However, if you are showing up as "low value," telling a man that you don't value or love yourself, and if he observes you treating yourself in that manner, how will he ever respect you? You've given him permission to treat you as you treat yourself. My loves, we must teach others how to handle us with care, dignity, and respect, and the only way that happens is if we have self-love, dignity, and respect for ourselves. #Nogreenbeans

I'm inclined to believe that we really do not know men, how to deal with them, and how to reach them as much as we think we do. Some women are experts in sleeping with men in exchange for monetary stability and for what they can get out of him and that's the extent.

Some women know how to have a man at their beck and call and know what to say and do to get him to a certain point. *What's the thought process behind my inclination?* Because if we understood all of "who men are," then it would challenge us to present all of "who we are."

I'll use "soul food" metaphorically. It's the heritage and culture of African Americans; however, that doesn't mean that every African American man desires to consume fried chicken, collard greens, and mac 'n' cheese if you are preparing a meal for him. It's important to understand and get to know what "he" likes and not assume, as he may have a different preference.

In the same way, precious jewels, not all men find it attractive, sexy, or "confident" for a woman to, blatantly or subliminally, offer herself for sexual pleasure. My loves, you can't possibly think you'll ever be more than a "side of green beans" in his eyes, because he has already conquered. There was no challenge for him. He's bored now. He's figured you out. This is when we typically label the man as being "no good." My gem, he may be good, but just not for you, as you've yet to discover how to leverage your dimensional value to have him desiring more of who you are, not what you do to him.

Remember, loves, the "Ultimate 5-Course Woman" is attentive while assessing. She's not studying a man to find his vulnerable areas so that he can be taken advantage of, manipulated, or used. She's doing assessment to learn him, and once she learns him from a pure place—not a place of manipulation and/or selfish gain—she's eventually able to identify the pathway to his heart, not his bedroom, her kitchen, or a hotel room. #Nogreenbeans #NGB

You have no idea how many of my friends tell me that they literally have to push women away, translated to turning away sex.

My beautiful jewels, the purpose of this chapter is not to influence you on how to use the "Power of the P," but to shift your mindset and introduce you to a different type of influence, which is "Positive

Persuasion." I mean after all, you have this transformational tool to become that "Ultimate 5-Course Experience": the type of experience that real men desire, pursue, and capture *(wink)*.

We discussed the irresistible influence of a sexual encounter; let's now discuss the irresistible influence of positive persuasion of a women who uses her influence on a man as a tool to build him and her.

My loves, can I share something with you? When we value ourselves, we project value, then everyone in our sphere of influence benefits. As we all know, as the world turns, so do the people in the world.

There is a different level of value that men place upon women who aren't co-dependent. Well…not men who are insecure, controlling, and narcissistic; they actually prefer you to be co-dependent on them—in fact, will overcompensate with gifts and the like to get you conditioned. They won't rent or purchase a home because they desire it; they will want you to move out of your place, so they offer somewhere that they consume the expenses. Let's be clear, they won't move in <u>with</u> you; they will just carry the expenses. So, they can still be at liberty but lock you down at the same time. *Why?* To control you and the situation. This generally happens when the man is married, lives with another woman, or just simply wants to "Pay-the-Cost-to-be-the-Boss." My loves, please, I beg of you… *#Nogreenbeans*

There is also a different value that women place on men who don't only desire sexual gain and pleasure. Men who can treat a lady like a lady. What happens when a woman who understands her value, is financially self-sufficient, and isn't needy comes into contact with a man who is used to "paying" to have his way? On the contrary, what happens when a woman who is used to sleeping with men for personal gain encounters a man that isn't as concerned with who she is in bed than with what's in her brain? What I've noticed is that neither the man nor the woman knows what to do. They are forced out of their comfort zones. It's easy to give money and sex in exchange, however, not for women *(both hands raised)* who aren't concerned with a man's monetary portfolio more that the respect she's shown while in his presence. Likewise, there are kings and priests that aren't as concerned with a sexual encounter.

You in demand: you're a rare commodity. We know how easy it is for men to have a different woman for a "different experience"— one woman will treat them like a king ... another will speak to the king IN them ... another will be their homie ... another will give them the ultimate sexual experience ... another will challenge them mentally ... another will hold him accountable, which they need and desire (not all).

Why am I speaking on this? Because men really desire the "Ultimate 5-Course Experience." They really have additional needs and desires besides sex. If it was sex that men valued, they wouldn't pay for it with a stranger and never see her again. If it was sex that men valued, it wouldn't be such a challenge to be in a monogamous relationship.

My challenge is for you to discover your value so that you can present your value. Your value determines your rating — when you know your value, it goes up. I'll be the first to tell you, "Yes, I'm costly but priceless.... I'm not sold to the highest bidder.... The value that my process, experience, and expertise has yielded is worth far more than designer bags, exquisite trips, and financial stability."

Men desire and appreciate authenticity. Don't be plastic; be who you are. Believe it or not, men are really impressed with the "real you" because that's who they become the best of friends with...that's who they fall in love with...that's who they can tell secrets to and be safe...that's who they will allow to be a voice in their lives and hold them accountable.

Gems and jewels, our kings and priests need us to place a demand on the king in them...and not the pig. Cause them to arise to another level by telling them "no." *Why?* Because he's in your sphere of positive persuasion, which is attractive.

My loves, we do a disservice to our gift of influence on the man when we scheme, deceive, and seduce rather than support, affirm, and build. Do we even know "how" to build up a man? Do we know how to speak positive words of affirmation that make him feel that he can conquer <u>anything</u>? Yes, it's true; it's the power of positive persuasion.

What is your function to a man? Do you know his to you? What's your strategy and intention? It may be in your best interest to assess so that you won't find yourself going in circles and/or at dead ends.

My loves, our intention and strategy should be to "Create a space" in him! It doesn't matter who he's been with; it doesn't matter how many times he's been in love. I don't care how deeply he's been in love. Our function and responsibility should be to "create a space" in him that is untouched, untapped, and unparalleled. Pay close attention in this area, my gems, and <u>assess</u>. Please don't try and "create a space" where you're constantly hitting a brick wall because he's emotional unavailable.

My loves, I have a question, "Have you ever offered sex and have been turned down?" I don't need an answer, but I know many women who have. How do I know this? Because of the results from my "Real Men–Real Answers" survey. I've heard many, many men say that they've turned down sex because the women (although beautiful with more beautiful bodies) were too loose, free, and overbearing. Some may ask, "What man turns down sex?" Several men will; men that are processed, mature, disciplined, and focused. There are men that simply desire more than the shallow experience of a sexual encounter.

Precious jewels, a man's thought process is that if we are quick to <u>offer</u> (translated "lack of value") our precious, prized possession without him getting the chance to know you or even the chance to deserve that dimension, you are doing the same with other men. They don't view it as, "Oh, she really likes me." They look at us as "a side of green beans," and immediately, we are placed in that category. You, my love, have positioned yourself as such and not the "Ultimate 5-Course Experience" that you are.

Jewels, please put me on auto repeat… "Men <u>need</u> a challenge." As a matter of fact, they like challenges because they are built for the chase—not the chase where he's showing interest and you aren't. I'm speaking of the chase where he's not able to have you at will…the chase where you establish <u>and</u> execute boundaries…the chase where you give him a gentle but firm "no" or "not yet." That's why men are so competitive; it's manufactured <u>in</u> them.

If men know already that they can have it easily, they *(well…some)* don't want it because it alleviates the chase and hunt that they are <u>built</u> for!!

My precious Queens let's commit to using the power of the P, which is the Power of Positive Persuasion.

Whipped Cappuccino

(After Dinner Reflection)

Gems & Jewels, we've enjoyed a delightful, consistent experience and now it's time for reflection while sipping a steamed & whipped cappuccino. Just as each course is intended to ignite further desire, we must "proportion" ourselves in such a way that men have no other choice than to see the depth and dimension of who we "really" are through a consistent experience which yields desire.

Remember, each new course you present will require a change in his palate! Precious queens, I admonish you to not allow men who are patterned to absorb fast food in the drive through to treat you as such. You must **require** that any man worthy of your "experience" realizes that you're worth faaaar more than a brown paper bag that he can grab quick, consume, and then toss in the trash when he's finished or if he's a reckless driver, toss out the window (see navigation system).

Five course dining requires "an experience" and you my love are the Ultimate! Don't you DARE allow a man to feast on your "Course 3" before he's experienced the dimensions that prepares him for the rest of you.

Please don't allow yourself to be generalized with "everyone else". When a man comes to you, he comes with learned behavior of not only his history, but a pattern of what's ALWAYS worked and it's your responsibility to separate yourself. You control the temperature.

It takes discipline (trained palate) and patience to resist the temptation of going through the drive through when there is full course meal at home. Men oftentimes know what they desire in a woman, but because the "5 Course Woman" is a rarity, they often "go with the flow" because she's the majority. Ladies don't be his only option of availability. Don't be his alternative, the one he comes to ONLY when what he really desires isn't available.

This writing and the tools herein are a process, there's no magic wand, despite the "Manifest the Love you Want" trend; darlings if we don't first manifest inner healing, then only toxicity and dysfunctional cycles with manifest, hence the reason assessment is a critical foundational tool because my love you will never be enough for the wrong person. Women of value understand their time is a commodity, therefore she safeguards it. You must do initial and continual assessment to determine if the man is ready for depth and dimension. Some men just aren't ready #period. These tools nor your time are recommended to someone who doesn't value self or who you are.

Remember my love, you are a rarity, a once in a lifetime, not one in a million. You are a one and only, not one of many. You are a preferred choice, not an option.

When we become that Ultimate 5-course experience, there is no room in a man's space for anything else because he is satisfied and well nourished. Even if something else "looks good" He's had enough and can't consumer another thing (wink).

I've enjoyed our time together immensely! Let's show up in the dimensional experiences we were designed to be! (Hugs) #Nogreenbeans #NGB #Theultimate5courseexperience

Coaching & Signature Programs

Visit us
www.nogreenbeans.com

We'd Love to Hear from You!

Please leave us a review
www.amazon.com
support@nogreenbeans.com

Stay Connected!

Join our Mailing List
www.nogreenbeans.com
IG - @no.greenbeans
Facebook – No Green Beans

Hashtags to Use

#Nogreenbeans
#Theultimate5courseexperience
#NGB

Made in the USA
Columbia, SC
06 April 2022